PATRISTIC MONOGRAPH SERIES, NO. 6

DISCIPLINA NOSTRA
। ।
Essays in Memory of Robert F. Evans

Edited by

Donald F. Winslow

Published by

The Philadelphia Patristic Foundation, Ltd.

1979

GG4
D 631

TABLE OF CONTENTS

i

PREFACE

Upon hearing of the death of Robert Evans,
Cyril Richardson wrote me a short note in which he
said, simply: "A great loss. A real scholar. A delightful conversationalist. He had a real gift for
charming style."

The "great loss" was felt by us all. And to
it was added the loss felt at Cyril Richardson's
death two years later. It is fortunate however that
Richardson was able to complete his contribution to
the memorial volume for Evans, for the two were intimate friends, respected each other's scholarship,
and shared many common interests.

The title for this volume of essays was
suggested by Richard Norris, Richardson's successor
at Union Theological Seminary; it is a phrase from
Tertullian and symbolizes both the commitment to
a "disciplined" life enjoined upon all Christians
as well as the common "discipline" which the contributors to this volume share with Robert Evans, the
discipline of patristic scholarship of which he was
so carefully and painstakingly a practitioner. The
contributors to this volume, apart from their all
having known Evans as a friend, were related to him
in a variety of ways: some of them were University
colleagues; some shared with him common professional
pursuits; some studied under him as graduate students.

A few of us worked happily with Evans in the formation of the Philadelphia Patristic Foundation, Ltd.,
of which he was co-founder and principal supporter.
His dream was to see first-rate works published in
the Foundation's Patristic Monograph Series. Since
his death precluded the fulfillment of that dream,
it seemed appropriate to have this memorial volume
of essays published by the Foundation which he helped bring into existence and in a monograph series
for which he had such high hopes.

It is with deep gratitude for the life of a
faithful friend and consummate scholar that these
essays are offered. It is because of this abiding
gratitude that these essays form as much a Fest-
schrift as they do a memorial volume.

Donald F. Winslow,
Editor

Episcopal Divinity School
Cambridge, Massachusetts
June, 1979

ROBERT FRANKLIN EVANS

SCHOLAR, TEACHER, AND UNIVERSITY CITIZEN

AN APPRECIATION

Robert Franklin Evans suffered a fatal heart attack on 30 May 1974 while jogging on a golf course during a visit to his parents' home in Aurora, Ohio. At forty-four years of age, his scholarly life was cut off in full bloom, and at a time when it promised to produce even greater fruit. His death was especially shocking because so unexpected. Although he had been under treatment for two years for what seemed to be a relatively mild angina condition, his discovery of jogging as a replacement for earlier forms of exercise, despite his physician's ambivalence as to its value, seemed to have produced beneficial results. He claimed to be feeling quite fit because of the exercise, and although his hair had turned prematurely gray a few years earlier, in external appearances he seemed to be as healthy and vigorous as ever that fatal spring of 1974.

Robert Evans' death left a wide and varied circle of mourners--his immediate family, including his wife Lilian and their daughters Danielle and Nicole; the church related world of friends, associates, colleagues, especially the clergy and parishioners from St. Mary's Episcopal Church where he had been organist, choirmaster and frequent preacher for the past thirteen years; students and faculty from the nearby Philadelphia Divinity School; the University of Pennsylvania community of students, colleagues, and associates who knew him in various connections; and the wider scholarly world of humanistic research and the study of religion in which Evans had distintuished himself as an outstanding member. How he appeared and how he saw himself in these various contexts, and what he accomplished in each, would require an essay far exceeding the ambitions of this one, and would necessarily draw upon resources not readily available to the present authors. Hoping, however, not to overlook those areas with which we are unfamiliar, we will attempt to focus on those facets of his life known to us through our association with him as a colleague and friend in the Department of Religious Thought at the University of Pennsylvania where his interaction with the educational and academic worlds was one in which we shared.[1]

Early Life and Formal Education

Robert Franklin Evans was born on 9 January 1930 in Akron, Ohio. His father, Charles Robert Evans was a buyer for Republic Steel Corporation and his mother, Lola Boyd, taught music at Western Reserve Academy in Hudson, Ohio. The family also included Robert's younger sister, Lavonne.

Music, and especially church music, was a central influence in young Robert's life. He began to play the paino at four years of age and had become organist at the Hudson Congregational Church by the age of thirteen. He received his High School Diploma from the Academy in which his mother taught, and spent the next four years earning his BA degree at Yale University (1951). He distinguished himself as a student at Yale, being named to Phi Beta Kappa, the Torch Honor Society, and the Elihu Senior Society. After graduation from Yale, Evans received a Fulbright Scholarship to pursue his musical interests in England at King's College, Cambridge. It was there that his future was significantly changed by two very different circumstances. First, he met and fell in love with Lilian Alder, a Swiss student studying English in Cambridge. Second, he developed a heretofore latent interest in the study of theology, and in particular church history, as a career possibility. He was, as he phrased it later, "bitten by the patristic bug."

Continuing his study of music, and embarking upon a rigorous study of the history of Christian thought, Evans earned his BA from King's College in 1955 (with the largely automatic MA following in 1961).

His honors included the Ehrman studentship (1952-54) and various theological scholarships. Increasing contact with Professor Henry Chadwick and others doubtless helped the bright young American to focus his patristic interests and to hone his academic abilities to a fine edge. When he returned to Yale as a doctoral candidate in 1955, the difficult choice between career goals had long been made--music had been replaced at center stage by patristic theology. At Yale, Evans worked chiefly under the direction of Professor Robert Lowry Calhoun and produced a dissertation on Four Letters of Pelagius which, after extensive revision, was published in 1968. He also performed impressively in two courses at Yale with Claude Welch, a fact that would become important later when Welch became chairman of the fledgling Department of Religious Thought at the University of Pennsylvania. At Yale, too, honors came to Evans; he received the distinguished Sterling Graduate Fellowship and was also elected a Kent Fellow by the Society for Religion in Higher Education. He was awarded his PhD in the spring of 1959.

It was while Evans was persuing his graduate studies at Yale that Lilian Alder joined him in New Haven where, in 1956, they were married. Two years later, the Evanses moved to Washington, D.C. Robert became canonically affiliated with the Episcopal Diocese of Washington and was subsequently ordained Deacon and then Priest in the Episcopal Church by Bishop Angus Dun. From 1958-60 he served as Assistant to the Rector of St. Thomas' Church. These church and parochial involvements would remain important to Evans for the remainder of his life as he enthusiastically continued his career in church music, preached often and widely, and participated in a variety of church educational undertakings.

In April 1959, as Evans' doctoral dissertation was being processed at Yale, Lilian gave birth to a daughter, Danielle. Two years later, in Philadelphia, a second daughter, Nicole would join the family.

Robert Evans' full-time academic teaching duties began with his appointment as an Instructor in the Department of Philosophy and Religion at Western Michigan University in Kalamazoo for the 1960/61 school year. He taught a wide range of subjects, including Introduction to Religion, Representative Christian Thinkers, Understanding the Old Testament, and a general education course called Arts and Ideas in which he was able to combine creatively his interest in music with his training in history and theology. Meanwhile, Professor Claude Welch came to the University of Pennsylvania with a mandate to develop an undergraduate and graduate program in Religious Studies. One of Welch's first major actions was to offer Evans a position in the Department. As Welch later stated in recommending Evans for a post-doctoral fellowship (December, 1964):

> I have known Robert Evans since his graduate study at Yale. At that time I was much impressed both by his previous preparation and by the quality of his work for me. My judgment of his work and his potentialities is indicated by the fact that he was the first appointment to our department to be made after my assumption of responsibilities as chairman at Penn.

The decision to leave Western Michigan University after so short a time for the new Program at Penn was not an easy one. A letter written to Welch in March of 1961 is indicative of the kind of integrity, honesty, and soul-searching that would characterize the whole of Evans' life:

> After much cogitation and introspection I have decided that I wish to accept your invitation to join the faculty of your department. . . The issue posed itself to me as a decision between relative ease and security [at WMU] on the one hand, and challenge and excitement, if more demanding, on the

4

other. It is clear to me that such a position as I might occupy at Penn is more in line with my long range interests, and it is also clear to me that I should not expect such an offer to come my way at just the moment I want it. . . . I look forward greatly to my association with you.

The association of Robert Evans with the University of Pennsylvania proved to be a lasting and happy one, albeit not without tensions, and his presence was to be extremely important to the development of the department. During his initial year as "Lecturer" (1961/62), there came from the College Dean the inevitable request in which it was stated that the University sought "more concrete assurance regarding the publication of his research results."[2] As it turns out, Evans did publish a major article in the Journal for Theological Studies and had yet another article accepted for publication. Thereupon Welch recommended him for promotion to Assistant Professor effective 1962/63, stating in his recommendation that "I certainly envision for him a permanent place in the department and a large role in our future work." The promotion was approved as a standard three-year appointment and was renewed for a second term in 1965. It was during these years that Evans also became increasingly involved in University activities beyond the confines of his Department. He served as freshman advisor for the College in 1962/63 and was acting chairman of the Department for a brief period in 1964 when Welch was on leave. From 1964, he also served on the Executive Committee of the College, which dealt mainly with problems of an academic nature (unsatisfactory performance, honors, waiver of rules, etc.), and was the advisor for departmental undergraduate majors from 1964/65 through 1969/70.

In the summer of 1964, Evans received a faculty research grant which freed him from his usual summer teaching responsibilities and gave him the opportunity to begin revising his doctoral dissertation. He also applied successfully for a Lilly Post-Doctoral Fellowship from the Hazen Foundation for 1965/66, and spent

5

the time in Tübingen, Germany, working on his studies of Pelagius and attending the ecumenical seminar of Hans Küng and, briefly, the systematics seminar of Gerhard Ebeling, as well as the Ausländercolloquium led by Ernst Käsemann. Evans was enthusiastic about Küng, whom he described (in a letter of 24 February 1966) as "no doubt the most irenic, genuinely open theologian whom I have met here." He developed a friendship with Ulrich Wickert, a Privatdozent who had responded to a paper on Paul which Evans had presented in the colloquium. He was also impressed with Wolfgan Pannenberg whom he had heard briefly at Mainz. On the other hand, Evans found himself "continually at odds" with Käsemann's point of view and concluded that Ebeling, although a "learned man," was rather opaque and "primarily . . . an interpreter of Luther to our age," with a "firm commitment to declare that Luther still speaks" (letters of 2/66 and 2/67). Evans was not opposed to such an apologetic approach, but seemed to resent finding it veiled in what posed as a more "objective" hermeneutic interest.

This period was not without its problems. Evans found himself frequently frustrated by the tension between his perfectionist scholarly standards and ideals, his variegated interests, and the realities and pressures which surrounded him at the University. He found it increasingly difficult to find time for his own research. He regularly did his work at his University office, but this made him all the more vulnerable to the whims of students who ignored his scheduled office hours and who might knock on his door at any time. It was with a real sense of relief and anticipation, then, that he looked forward to his summer research fellowship in 1964: "The prospects of three solid months of research is a most pleasing one" (letter of 4/64). He continually attempted to resist those real or imagined pressures which would have him sacrifice quality for the sake of building up an impressive list of publications in order to secure promotion and tenure. The depth of his feelings on this matter are clearly revealed in an impassioned letter to the Department Chairman in early 1965, a letter in which he juxtaposed with precision his scholarly ambitions with his own self-image:

> This . . . problem . . . is primarily a per-
> sonal one, although I think that at least one
> aspect of my own problem is part of a larger,
> "American" problem. I am interested in patris-
> tic studies, as you know, and have chosen to
> make that my own area of special study and re-
> search. I am not interested in the publication
> of second and third rate scholarship--at least
> I am not interested in publishing noticeably
> below the level of which I believe I am capa-
> ble. I believe right now that my total publish-
> ed work will in the end amount to a rather
> modest corpus, and this because of the limita-
> tions of my own background and ability. I wish
> and intend to publish, but my publication must
> proceed at my own rather limping rate. At Yale
> I made an intense effort to finish my doctoral
> dissertation within two years after I began
> it, and now I know how bad a job I did. The
> research grant I had in the summer of 1964
> gave me the leisure to discover how shoddy
> was the work I had done, and I have scarcely
> yet recovered from that revelation. I just do
> not want to feel the pressure of having to
> get out a certain amount of stuff over the
> next couple of years, and equally do I not
> want to cause you any embarrassment when the
> question of my promotion comes up in the spring
> of 1967. I am hoping, therefore, to find, over
> the next three years, an associate professor-
> ship with tenure at a college or seminary. It
> may be that after a dozen or so years of work
> in that kind of environment I would be able
> to return to a University professorship. It
> may also be that the environment which I am
> now seeking will be the one in which I will
> wish to stay. That can remain an open issue.

If these concerns give evidence of a feeling of
professional insecurity, they appear to have been
wholly personal and internal, for there were certainly

no departmental pressures being brought to bear, nor
any indication within the University that Evans' promotion to tenure was in the least problematical. The
letter continues:

> Allow me to make a few observations on the
> larger problem as I see it, and as I see my
> relation to it. When one enters patristic
> studies, one enters a tradition of scholar-
> ship. For my studies, this means primarily
> a tradition that comes immediately from Eur-
> ope--from Germany, Britain, and France. The
> models of scholarship that I inevitably take
> to heart are models formed by German Univer-
> sity professors, Oxford and Cambridge dons,
> and French Benedictines and Jesuits. Now, by
> and large, when these people have undertaken
> the enterprise of Dogmengeschichte, they
> have done so on the basis of a classical edu-
> cation which they have assimilated in Gymna-
> sium, Public School followed by Oxford or
> Cambridge, and monastic school, respectively.
> One of Adolph von Harnack's cardinal princi-
> ples was that the science of Dogmengeschichte
> must be built upon the solid foundation of
> philological learning and textual criticism,
> and he was right. And of course he assumed
> a wide knowledge of ancient history as well.
> American doctoral candidates in historical
> theology come to their studies on the basis
> of a theological interest nurtured usually
> in seminary (an atmosphere with no notable
> bias toward classical studies), with God
> knows what kind of emphasis behind them in
> their college and secondary education, and
> proceed immediately to the history of theo-
> logical ideas, without the classical sub-
> structure (of course I am talking about what
> usually happens, not about what sometimes
> happens, and I am talking about myself).
> This, I am persuaded, is at least one
> very important reason why American output in
> patristic studies is so unimpressive, in both

quantity and quality. . . The American would-
be patristic scholar is given a graduate training largely in the history of ideas and has to
pick up classical learning on the way somewhere,
if he picks it up at all. Some of us find this
more difficult than others, by the time we are
in our thirties.

I have to confess that I find it difficult--
difficult at best and particularly difficult in
the midst of many other pressing duties. It is
not that one has to despair or give up--one
does not easily give up, having been bitten by
the patristic bug. It is just that I, for one,
have to go slowly. I now believe that I will
have the inner freedom to go ahead with my professional studies in an environment in which
there is no sense of a deadline to be met in
order that I may stay. If I cannot find an
associate professorship with tenure in a college or seminary, I shall return to parish work.
. . . At worst, one could say that I want the
security which will allow me to be plodding and
mediocre; I hope that is not true. At best, one
could say that I want the freedom to put out
the best stuff of which I am capable, at my own
rate; I hope something more like this is the
case. . . I am sorry . . . that I was not able
to see these things clearly long ago. It goes
without saying, of course, that with my present intentions, I shall be unable to accept
the Lilly award if I get it.

Fortunately, Evans did receive the Lilly award
and was able to find a way to accept it without compro-
mising his integrity, steering a middle path between
his once articulated "intentions" and the realities of
University life. By mid-1967, his two volumes on Pelagius were complete and accepted for publication. Evalu-
ations of his scholarly work by specialists and colleagues both here and abroad were consistently enthusiastic, so much so that they assured his being promoted to Associate Professor with tenure. The departmental recommendation by Claude Welch aptly summed up the

situation:

> Evans has the equipment, energy, commitment,
> and discipline appropriate to his scholarly
> position and responsibilities. His publica-
> tions, though small in number, are superb in
> quality, and a continued flow of similar ef-
> forts is expected from him. His horizons of
> academic interest are wide, including philo-
> sophy of religion[3] as well as the history of
> western thought in general and Christian pa-
> tristics in particular. He is a committed and
> respected teacher, 'well liked by all students
> who are prepared to accept the demands he
> places on them.' He is a 'constructive and
> helpful' departmental colleague who has been
> 'serving effectively' as director of the un-
> dergraduate departmental major program.

Needless to say, the promotion was quickly approved
in May 1967, providing Evans, for all his self-doubts,
with the professional "security," and thus to some extent the personal "freedom," to proceed in his scholarly contributions at his own pace.

The Tenured Teacher/Scholar in a Time of Unrest and Change

The latter part of the 1960's, between Evans'
first sabbatical in 1965/66 and his second in 1970/71,
was a time of notable unrest within the University at
large and of significant changes within the small but
relatively flourishing Religious Thought Department.
Evans found himself involved in the changing climate
in a variety of directions. In the mid-1960's, the
College created a special "General Honors" program
geared for especially talented undergraduates--one of
the first of special programs aimed at providing,
among others things, closer contact between students
and teachers. When Evans returned from his first sabbatical in 1966, he agreed to offer a General Honors
course on "The Religious Roots of Western Culture"

10

and found the experience sufficiently satisfying that
he agreed to serve as Associate Director of the General Honors Program from 1967-70, and regularly offered
courses in that program to the end of his life. He also
became involved in the special "Freshman Seminars" program in the early 1970's.

Meanwhile, the questions about the structure and
aims of both the undergraduate and graduate programs
in Religious Thought were being raised, especially by
the students. As the departmental advisor for undergraduate majors, Evans chaired a committee for the
revision of the curriculum. In this role, he was conscientiously active in the department's attempts to
adjust to the increasingly urgent requests made by
graduate students for more active participation in departmental affairs. During this same period, he served
once again as acting chairman of the department during
Welch's leave of absence in 1968, and also began a
long and active role on the College Admissions Committee, of which he was appointed chairman in 1969/70 and
again in 1971/72.

Evans' concern for maintaining high standards
of quality education appears again and again in the
records from this period. But there also appears what
might be called a "humanizing" tendency in Evans' outlook for all his insistence on high standards. There
was the desire always to be open to the ideas and experiences of others, to see students as people, not
defining them exclusively in their academic contest.
Certain old barriers, which had previously created a
distance between Evans and others, came down, and there
emerged a refreshing openness and cheerfulness, indicating perhaps not so much a new way of doing things
as an increased confidence in himself. One small but
visible symbol of this is that, whereas in earlier
years it was not uncommon for Evans to wear his clerical collar even when teaching, this habit gradually
disappeared.[4] In the same vein, Evans had previously
expressed some concern about the increasing number of
women applying to the graduate program. But he soon
realized that his doubts as to their ability to pursue scholarly goals was a culturally conditioned reaction and he became an articulate spokesman for the

argument that it would be both irresponsible and immoral
for the department to take any notice of gender in evaluating applications. (Evans' vigorous sermons in St. Mary's
Church advocating the ordination of women were further
testimony to the seriousness with which he fought against
age old prejudices in both academic and ecclesial circles.)
It was not merely a social facade, then, when Evans could
point out to "unbelievers" that some of the most promising
and competent, as well as most pleasant, students in the
graduate programs were in fact women.

The advancement to tenure which gave Evans the
"freedom" to pursue his own research at his own pace,
also freed him to take an increasingly involved role in
a variety of University circles. His exposure to young
people seeking admission to the College, his work with
those whose work was unsatisfactory (Executive Committee) and those whose work was exemplary (General Honors
Program); his contacts with an increasingly variegated
circle of University faculty and administration--all
these factors contributed to the make-up of the Robert
Evans who sought to define and modify his position
among the pressures and changes of the late 1960's. It
was an experience from which both he and the Deaprtment
profited greatly!

The Mature Scholar/Teacher and Departmental Leader

In 1970/71 Robert Evans received a cross-disci-
linary fellowship from the Society for Religion in
Higher Education to study Roman Law, Stoicism, and
Middle Platonism in Vienna, Austria, (He remarked more
than once that the academic resources of that city
were equalled, if not surpassed, by its musical and
gustatory attractions!) His application for the grant
affords illuminating insights into how he had come, in
comparison to his previous self-doubt, to view his
own ambitions and accomplishment:

> My research and writing over the past de-
> cade have moved from a rather restricted
> area of precise scholarship to broader
> areas of increasing generality. The field

12

of research in which I work is that of ancient Christian thought and literature. . . My research on the Pelagian controversy brought me to the early conclusion that one of the most fundamental issues at stake was that of the nature of the Christian Church. . . This line of reflection then led me to agree to the request of a publisher to write a book on the development of thought about the Church in Western theology from the third through the sixth century. . . Having thus come from a very detailed and small-scale philological exercise to a treatment of the development of thought over a period of four centuries, I think I must now make a move which will at one and the same time be a return to details and make plausible the kind of broader ranging, more comprehensive, scholarship in which I am more basically interested. It has for some time been apparent, at least to the better scholars in the field, that studies in the history of Christianity have long suffered from "underdevelopment" in the use of the normal methods and resources of the historian. That is to say that the history of Christian institutions and of Christian thought has been too much viewed as an intramural history, a history that can be grasped simply as the continuous history through time of a single society, the Christian Church. This way of viewing the history of Christianity (and the history of other religions as well) has brought abundant distortions; it has kept us in needless ignorance of the actual significance of religious institutions and thought by obscuring their relations and parallels to the wider society, or culture, within which they emerge. In my own field specifically this means that the patristic scholar should be conversant with the relevant aspects of classical culture as a whole.

I have cause to sense this challenge in a particular and personal way. My own undergraduate education, with a music major, included only one course in classical studies. My graduate education was largely theological in orientation, and while in one sense I do not regret that orientation, I am sensible of the fact that I did not come to my field of research from the background of classical studies which would have best equipped me for the research in which I am now engaged and in which I want to be more profoundly and fruitfully engaged.

My proposal, then, is for a year of detailed study in classical sources, both Latin and Greek. . . My study will be oriented toward the future research and publication which I intend to carry out as well as toward the kind of graduate seminars that I have recently taught and intend to teach. This future writing and teaching will include the whole course, over a century and beyond, of the Pelagian controversy, as well as studies of such pivotal figures in the patristic period as Cyprian, Origen, Jerome, and Augustine. My study in classical sources, therefore, will be chiefly if not wholly concerned with the following three areas: 1) Roman imperial law, a subject of the greatest importance for the vocabulary of Christian life and institutions in the patristic period, particularly in view of the way in which many patristic authors viewed the Church as an alternative society to that of the Roman empire, though a society employing terms borrowed from the institutions of that empire; 2) Roman stoicism, a subject closely related both to the development of Western Christian thought about the nature of man, his freedom, and his true good; 3) middle-Platonic and neo-Platonic philosophy, a subject indispensable to an understanding, for example, of two such seminal figures as Origen and Augustine.

It is important to emphasize that the program of study which I have in mind will be different from such study of these sources in which I have already been engaged. Heretofore I have always begun with the Christian authors,

14

and as questions and hunches have occurred to
me, I have gone to the non-Christian sources
by way of looking up answers to those particular
questions. Now I want to begin with the non-
Christian sources themselves, with the suspicion that I may find materials there which will
enable me to set the Christian sources in new
perspective that I have not gained in proceed-
ing the other way round.

When Evans returned to Penn in 1971/72, a new
situation had developed which was to engage and sometimes frustrate him for his remaining years. Claude
Welch had left the University and was succeeded as
chairman by Van Harvey (who had come to Penn in 1968/69
and had been serving for the past two years as the departmental director of graduate studies). Evans now
agreed to assume the duties of graduate chairman, in
addition to resuming the post of chairman of the College
Admissions Committee and also serving on the Executive
Committee of the University's College of General Studies (which administered the extension courses, night
school, etc.). Furthermore, some of the graduate students were clamoring for a reassessment of certain departmental requirements which they felt were unclear
and/or unfair. Too, the economic crises confronting the
University was producing pressures to cancel small graduate courses (because they were an economic luxury)
and to concentrate on increasing departmental undergraduate offerings and enrollments.
    The old frustrations concerning availability
for research time, the maintenance of academic standards, the application of sound pedagogical principles,
and similar concerns, all resurfaced in concert. To
the administration's suggestion that the department's
faculty might confine their graduate teaching to indi-
vidualized tutorials, Evans responded with characteristic vigor:

        I am firmly opposed to the notion that at the
        graduate level the dispensability of a man's
        formal courses is to be measured by the number
        of students . . . in his courses. . . . Graduate

teaching . . . is an expensive operation, and in my field it is especially so. . . [The administration's] proposal raises in my mind two further important questions: my own usefulness in the graduate faculty, and the standards of graduate education in the kind of field which is mine. On the first question, let me say that I am quite willing to confine my formal teaching to the undergraduate level. But [in that event] I would not be willing to do any graduate teaching, formal or informal. [This would be a severe disappointment because] one of the chief reasons for my coming here from Michigan was the promise of graduate teaching. It would of course be possible for me to increase the number of graduate students I teach by setting lower standards. . . I am simply unwilling to give graduate students credit for patristic courses taken with me on any assumption other than graduate work in patristics is work with sources in their original languages. . . The issue of teaching load is one that opens up a host of problems which mutually involved all members of the department and which concerns matters of standards in graduate teaching. . .

Although a reasonable compromise was reached between the departments and the University regarding minimal size of graduate seminars, this and other factors led to a decline in the number of graduate seminars offered by Evans thereafter. He did accept into his seminars qualified students from other deparments of the University or from the Philadelphia Divinity School, but the numbers were always low. This conflict between quantity (numbers) and quality (education) continued to be a source of frustration, particularly because Evans was unwilling to compromise either his own integrity as a scholar/teacher or those standards of excellence which he believed defined the level of graduate education.
Fortunately, there were compensating developments which gave Evans the opportunity to participate in and contribute to scholarly undertakings beyond the

confines of the University. As early as the spring of 1968 the New York Patristics Seminar was formed, with Evans as a charter member. Scholars from colleges, universities, and seminaries met monthly to share and discuss their research, and Evans found this a happy outlet both for his professional interests as well as for his desire for increased social contacts. Evans participated too in the work of the Philadelphia Seminar on Christian Origins and is remembered for the lively but always judicious criticisms which he brought to bear on the topics under discussion. As a result of a suggestion made originally by Claude Welch, some formalization of relations with the Philadelphia Divinity School was undertaken, resulting in the joint offering of courses in the field of patristics by Evans, Richard Norris and Donald Winslow. Of exceptional interest to Evans at this time was the gradual formation of the Philadelphia Patristic Foundation of which he and Winslow were co-founders. Consonant with Evans' high ideals for patristic scholarship was his dismay that, because of spiralling costs in the publishing field, manuscripts of quality were no longer being accepted by commercial houses--often because of the technical requirements involved in the use of foreign languages and critical apparatus. And when manuscripts were accepted, they were being priced beyond the range of the normal student's ability to purchase them. Evans conceived of a plan whereby scholarly works in the field could be prepared in typescript and printed by photo off-set, on a non-profit basis, thereby reducing the cost and making sure that important studies could be made available to the academic world. It was thus that the Foundation gave birth to the Patristic Monograph Series, although, with the death of Evans and the merger of the Philadelphia Divinity School with the Episcopal Theological School in Cambridge the direct connection with Philadelphia is retained only in the name of the Foundation.

In the spring of 1973 a crisis over the structure of the PhD qualification requirements in the department influenced Evans to resign as graduate chairman. An experimental proposal to permit students to substitute other work for a traditional examination requirement was accepted by the department, after long debate and much revision, despite the various serious reservations expressed by Evans and others. In his mind it was, again, a matter of educational standards being jeopardized. His decision to resign was further motivated by the increasing demands made by the office of graduate chairman. In a long letter (4/73) to the acting chairman, he explained his decision:

> I believe that . . . a two or three year term [as graduate chairman] is all anyone should be expected to serve. The graduate chairman gets no relief in teaching load, and besides looking after internal graduate affairs has to occupy himself with problems of placement, which requires a great deal of correspondence . . . Since changes are being made in our graduate department with which I am not in sympathy, I think now is the time for a change. . . It is out of the questions that with my present beliefs I could serve as graduate chairman any longer with either confidence or zest. If the new program is to work as well as it might, it needs someone behind it who has both of these things.

Thus, after two years as chairman, Evans stepped down for what he considered to be the good of the department. In the remaining year prior to his death, he characteristically accepted what the department had agreed upon as its new set of rules and cooperated fully in the implementation of those rules. No hard feelings were evidenced. The battle had been fought and was over. The future lay ahead, and that was what mattered. But for him, it proved to be all too brief a future.

Robert Evans was promoted to the status of full professor effective July 1973. The supporting materials from colleagues and scholars throughout the world included such observations as these:

> His depth and breadth of knowledge are awesome at times; he is a meticulous worker who knows

his field and takes a 'no nonsense' approach to scholarship. He is anxious to learn from others as well as to share what he knows with others.

In the Department, he has been invaluable. . . I can always count on his advice and whatever he does, he does with a very high standard of responsibility and efficiency.

[He is] an extremely learned person, a knowledgeable and penetratingly critical scholar, especially in the area of early church history. . . Especially in this day and age, when there is a tendency to superficiality even in the arts/humanities, I find it to be an extraordinary prize to find a historically oriented scholar who is able to work on the original text using such basic linguistic skill.

He is a scholar of notable depth and range and has a capacity for writing English which is admirable. . . I have found him original in his approach as well as well founded in his discipline.

Evans is . . . one of the five or six most distinguished Americans working in his general field. . . He combines in an unusual way a capacity for exacting textual and philological work, a good nose for promising and fruitful problems, and a grasp of larger historical and philosophical issues.

He has almost all the qualities once associated with academic distinction and good colleagueship: he's a gracious, interesting conversationalist with great resources of knowledge and bibliography and yet also with a snarp, critical mind that reacts quickly to nonsense and inaccuracies (easy to talk to, difficult to con). [He] will keep alive a basic discipline and find younger scholars to train for its ongoing future.

These were not hollow words of praise and promise but find full support in all areas of Evans' abbreviated life and career. He was a scholar's scholar, a dedicated searcher in pursuit of knowledge, a talented specialist, and a person of versatile and wide-ranging knowledge. The expectations he placed on others were always expectations he took seriously for himself, which meant, of course, that he was not always appreciated by everyone. Undergraduate students would find him formidable, even at times intimidating, especially in the early years of his teaching. He was perceived by some to be excessively hard in grading and evaluating: "An A is a very hard grade to receive." Students were often awed at what struck them as an unnecessary attention to complicated detail. The more specialized or advanced a course was, however, the more students tended to respect Evans' gifts, to see him as a "brilliant lecturer" who made it possible for the student to become "interested, yes, even fascinated by the subject matter." And serious students soon discovered how seriously Evans took them and their own educational progress.[5]

Over the years, a large number of undergraduates were enrolled in his courses and encountered the broad spectrum of Evans' interests. Throughout his years at Penn, Evans taught the "Basic Concepts of Religion" course which dealt especially with the central problems posed in modern western philosophy of religion. Some 750 or more students passed through that course during the years Evans taught it. Students encountered Evans, too, in the frequent night courses he offered as well as in his regular summer school offerings in the College of General Studies. From 1961/62 through 1967/68, Evans also taught both halves of the introductory course, "Living Religions of the World." More in line with his specific interests were undergraduate offerings on "Christian Thought to the Reformation" and the afore-mentioned course on "Religious Roots in Western Culture." "Selected Great Books of Western Civilization" and "Life, Times and Thought of Augustine" also figured among his undergraduate courses. On

20

the graduate level, his interest in the philosophy of religion was indicated in a seminar he offered called "Types of Theism" and in another seminar on 18th century religious thought. Specialized work was focussed on second to fifth century patristic studies (especially Clement and Origen, Tertullian, Pelagius and Augustine). It was always a disappointment to him that so few graduate students shared his enthusiasm for the Latin fathers. One suspects that Evans would not have been discontent to conduct all his course and seminar work in that area. Yet those graduate students for whom Evans served as advisor recognized and appreciated the sense of mutual respect which was engendered by his dealings with them as well as his genuine concern for their academic pursuits even when in areas other than his beloved patristic studies.

Robert Evans among his Colleagues

Much has already been said about how much Evans meant to his colleagues, University associates and fellow scholars. In the broader University setting, he was a responsible and respected citizen in the Faculty of Arts and Sciences. He took his role here with extreme seriousness. He rarely missed a faculty meeting, and at those in which the assembled few gathered to discuss new course proposals or programs, it was not unusual for Evans to rise and, in addition to contributing some substantive comment, to chide the writers of the proposal for any lapses in grammar or other linguistic barbarisms. Beyond the University, apart from those activities which we have already described, Evans was involved in a wide variety of scholarly groups and societies--the Society for Religion in Higher Education, the Society for the Scientific Study of Religion, the American Academy of Religion (and as an editorial consultant for its Journal), and the Philadelphia Oriental Club. Shortly before his death he was notified that he had been elected to the prestigious American Theological Society, into which he would have been inducted in the spring of 1975. Groups closer to his field of interest included the

American Society of Church History and the North American Patristics Society. In open scholarly discussion he was constantly probing, searching for reasons and for the evidence behind a particular claim. Yet he was unpretentious in his learning, and even when he felt fairly sure of his criticism he tried, not always with success, to avoid taking what appeared to be a dogmatic or intimidating stance. A typical prelude to some devastating criticism from Evans would be some evident restlessness on his part as he sought the floor, followed by a politely impatient introduction such as "But--but, surely you don't mean to say . . . or perhaps you do?" In later years, Evans would deliver those lines with a bit more of an honest chuckle and a bit less exasperation than in younger days. But whatever his humane intentions, his forceful authorial voice and his somewhat stiff bearing often helped multiply the anxieties of the person being confronted, and underlined the seriousness of the criticism.

Robert Evans as Author

Although very much at home with the pen, and a rhetorician of consummate skill, Evans was, as we have already seen, slow and cautious to publish. His first serious attempts at publication reflect the two major foci of his life, music and patristics; he reviewed J. Blanton's The Organ in Church Design in the 1959 volume of the Journal of the American Institute of Architects and T. Bohlin's monograph of Pelagius in the Journal of Theological Studies (1959). A popular book entitled Making Sense of the Creeds was being prepared at the same time as his two Pelagius articles in 1962. The Yale dissertation, after extensive revision, was published (1968) as Four Letters of Pelagius; in this work he established that only four of the nineteen works attributed to Pelagius by the noted scholar Georges de Plinval can be proved to be authentic. The companion volume, entitled Pelagius: Inquiries and Reappraisals, treats a number of historical and theological problems relating to Pelagius, and especially calls for a revised estimate of the relation between

Pelagius and his chief opponent, Augustine of Hippo. A major product of Evans' 1970/71 sabbatical leave was the publication, in 1972, of his One and Holy: The Church in Latin Patristic Thought. This was a careful investigation of the development of theories concerning the church in western theology from the third to the sixth century. Also during this period, two related articles on Tertullian's ecclesiology were published, one of them originally presented as a "Master Theme" at the Sixth International Conference on Patristic Studies at Oxford, and was entitled, "On the Problem of Church and Empire in Tertullian's Apologeticum." Various book reviews and encyclopedia articles were completed as well, along with English translations of Latin and German materials. In later years, Evans began to prepare the groundwork for a major study of Augustine, a study to which he intended to devote the greater part of his research for several years to come. His death prevented him from pursuing this undertaking.

Robert Evans as a Person

There was a decidely "conservative" and "old style" tone to Evans' attitudes to scholarship and education. On the academic scene, at least, he was a powerfully formal person whose ingrained tendency was to distinguish clearly between the roles of student and teacher. He was a "private" person, very circumspect in his conversation, who seldom bared his personal feelings, even to the closest of his colleagues. His was a "literary" person for whom the security of expressing himself as clearly as possible in writing often outweighed whatever convenience oral communication might provide. Indeed, he often stated his preference that recommendations of students for departmental fellowships, etc., be available in writing, even if Evans himself or one of the other committee members were the recommender. The text is fixed; it is available for scrutiny; one can return to it in case of doubt or confusion. Memories are frail; the spoken word is often imprecise; people do not always mean what they say (or say what they mean to convey).

He was also partly deaf in his left ear, and thus did not always trust even his own hearing. In meetings as is conversations his head would be attentively tilted slightly to one side so as to assist his good ear to operate more efficiently, and requests from him for the speaker to repeat what was said (or resumés of what he understood to have been said) were not infrequent.

Robert Evans was a man of high principle, with a sharply defined idea of what constituted appropriate or inappropriate responses in a given situation. He expected promises to be honored, and he looked for consistency of action and attitude within a highly rational perspective. He abhorred sham or duplicity or weakness under pressure. He demanded honesty and a straight answer. There were, as a result, inevitable conflicts, with students and colleagues alike. If Evans felt he could not operate with a clear conscience within the framework imposed upon him, he would say so to the extent of contemplating resignation from the University or from some póst within it; if his principles seemed at odds with the situation confronting him, few people were left in doubt as to his views. He believed that the University should promote its faculty at the appropriate time on the basis of quality of performance without reference to whether a faculty member was considering an offer to teach elsewhere.[6] He was outraged by failures of others to operate within the framework of the established rules--whether it was a committee exceeding its mandate, or a graduate school offering fellowship money after the stipulated date for doing so had passed, or a faculty member changing a student's grade simply because of student or parent pressure, or an athlete receiving special treatment unavailable to every student. These attitudes extended even to seemingly minor matters. In the early years of the Philadelphia Seminar on Christian Origins of which Robert was a charter member in 1963, he would sometimes chide his office-mate and coordinator of the group for editing the "minutes" of the meetings so that they did not always record precisely what had been said by a participant, but attempted to correct any misstatements of fact or other minor lapses incidental to the main

24

line of the argument, thus presenting what <u>should</u> have been said if the speaker had been more aware of his subject or more careful with his speech. Evans' comments on the matter were partly delivered with tongue in cheek, and certainly without any personal malice, but nevertheless there remained a seriousness to the criticism, a seriousness arising out of his concern for academic honesty.

Yet, within this sometimes foreboding framework of thought and action, Robert Evans emerged as an eminently reasonable person, patient to hear and evaluate rational arguments offered by his peers, and true enough to his own principles to change his position if the counter-arguments seemed convincing. His stabilizing presence in the department and on the various programs and committees on which he served was much respected by his colleagues and much sought. This, of course, created further problems because of increasing demands made on his time--time which he highly coveted for his own scholarly research purposes.

Evans was a perfectionist who expected of himself as well as of others who claimed to be learned persons a kind of precision in knowledge and expression that is all too rare. (His desire to perfect his own skills sometimes had a direct, and not always beneficial, impact on his home life. For example, at one point he attempted to regularize a schedule in which dinner table conversation with his trilingual wife and young daughters would be conducted in French one night and in German the next--an enviable ideal that soon proved impracticable.) Among students and colleagues he was reserved and sparing in offering praise, so that even the slightest recognition of merit from him carried all the more weight. A younger colleague tells of soliciting Evans' reaction to a technical study published in a scholarly journal. After thoughtfully reading the colleague's manuscript, Evans handed it back with a rather matter-of-fact statement to the effect that "You sensed something was wrong and have followed it up effectively." Hardly lavish praise, but none was needed. If you knew Robert Evans, that was ample praise indeed. The job was worth doing and had been done satisfactorily. What more need be said? That is what sound scholarship is all about!

In social gatherings where no professional or academic matters were under consideration, Robert could be the soul of conviviality. Good food and good wine he appreciated boundlessly, as he did the intimacy of close friends. He possessed a delightful, if not always obvious, sense of humor and was blessed with the ability (under the right circumstances!) to laugh at himself. In the early 1970's, meetings of the Philadelphia Seminar of Christian Origins were normally followed by an informal social gathering at the apartment of Betsy Purintun, one of the Penn graduate students participating in the Seminar. On one such occasion, Evans arrived relatively late to find the room inhabited exclusively by graduate students, some of whom were chronologically his peers. "My God!" he blurted, with an explosive chuckle and gleaming eye, "Am I the only ADULT here?" At another time, in May of 1973, he penned a note to his colleague and former office-mate Bob Kraft as follows:

> If I mistake not, it is you who are to be thanked for elevating the standard of graffiti in the men's room on the fourth floor [of Duhring wing, where their respective offices were located]. You are to be congratulated both in respect to literary style and subject matter.

Kraft, unfortunately being innocent of the deed, took the earliest opportunity to discover what had so obviously tickled Evans' academic and theological funnybone. The words, he found, written in a fine flowing hand, were as follows:

> Robert Evans who's fond of Pelagius
> Finds predestination outrageous.
> There needn't have been
> Original sin --
> Bad habits are simply contagious!

Perhaps, as a foot-note to posterity, Kraft's poetic reply to Evans should also be recorded:

26

>At paleography you're not very hot.
>My writing it clearly is <u>not</u>!
>   For its doctrinal ken
>   In such neat flowing pen
>McInerney's the pundit, I wot.

Whether Lee McInerney, one of Evans' advanced graduate
students at the time, was indeed responsible for the
free-will verse will remain his secret. But it provided a pleasant interlude, and an interesting insight
into Robert Evan's personality.

     Robert's great obsession, other than scholar-
ship, was, as has been noted, music. These two activities seemed to be vehicles of expression for antitheti-
cal sides of his character. As an academician, he could
be rationalistic, preoccupied, somewhat pedantic and
austere. As a musician, however, he was improvisato-
rial, expressive, and often boyishly unreserved. A
friend once remarked after hearing Evans play the
organ at St. Mary's Episcopal Church and direct the
choir during a Sunday morning service, "Now I have
seen the <u>real</u> Bob Evans!" People who saw him only in
one context were frequently surprised to learn how he
was regarded in th other. As an academic, he frequently intimidated graduate and undergraduate students, and
the tensions that arose were especially painful to him.
He loved students, but he also believed that they sometimes were threatening that model of scholarship which
he so prized and with which he had identified himself.
Those of his friends who knew him more intimately found
him a warm and loyal friend, one who loved to talk and
drink late into the night and who could be, given the
proper setting, charmingly boisterous. There was even
deep within him a Romantic streak that only came to expression in his playing of the organ and in an occa-
sional revelation made to a friend. One such revelation was when, rather quaintly, he confessed to a
friend that every Christmas he read the nineteenth
century German Romantic <u>Dialogue on Christmas Eve</u> by
Friedrich Schleiermacher that celebrates family life
and friendship but which also ends with the view that
the only authentic response to great significant mo-

ments in life is not ."cold and rigid speech" but music!
It was through music that Robert expressed feelings he
seemed not to permit himself to do as an academic. The
pipe organ was his instrument par excellence, and he
played it with uncommon vigor, enthusiasm, and skill.
To those who could sometimes peek into the darken-
ed sanctuary of St. Mary's church on a Saturday af-
ternoon when he practiced, he seemed transformed.
Caught up in his playing, he appeared to be suspended
in mid-air--drawn upward by a prematurely grayed head
straining as though it wanted to leave his shoulders,
but pulled downwards by his feet working intricate
patterns on the pedal beneath the bench.

***

The various faces of Robert Evans--scholar,
musician, teacher, colleague, friend--reflect to a
large degree the paradox between strongly held ideals
and ever-present realities. Evans was plagued by this
problem to the very end, as is patent from these words
of his written in late February 1974.

I write . . . in some considerable internal
rage, directed . . . in large part at myself. I have come to the realization that
I am really very unsatisfied with the kind
of life that I am leading from 8 a.m. to
6 p.m. most every day of the month. In part
I am myself responsible for my present discontent, in that I have not been sufficiently
prudent and provident with respect to my own
basic interests and goals. I have allowed
myself to be malleable in the hands of others
and have not had the courage often enough to
say no to requests and demands made of me.
The chief reason for my entering academic
life was my interest in scholarship, research, and writing. I am at the moment not
doing enough of these things to keep me
going on an even keel. My inability in past
months to say no to people is a personal
problem that I have got to work on myself.

28

To what extent Robert Evans would have been successful in attaining his ideals will never be known. His absence is the reality with which we must live. But he leaves us a legacy and a challenge--the pursuit of rigorous scholarship in a circumspect humanistic setting combined with a desire to understand ourselves and those with whom we work. May we never have to turn our backs on those ideals.

Robert A. Kraft

with Van A. Harvey

The Episcopal Theological Seminary of the Southwest
Austin, Texas

THE EXEGESIS OF I JOHN 3.19-20

AN ECUMENICAL MISINTERPRETATION?

It would be difficult to find two verses of scripture which have given the commentator, especially the modern one, more embarassment than these. They bristle with difficulties. When, moreover, after straining every point of grammar and meaning, the exegete has arrived at an acceptable sense, he despairingly encounters the fact that this sense is so curiously out of context. Where we expected some clue by which to know whether we are of the truth, we seem diverted into a digression on scruples of conscience. Hans Windisch, after offering a not too ingenious correction of the text, ironically adds, "But the best thing, to be sure, is to abide by the assertion that the text is corrupt."[1] C. H. Dodd, on the other hand, less addicted than the Germans to emending the text, lays all the trouble at the author's own door. He writes: "This brief section (19-24) consists of a series of loosely connected statements, set forth briefly and boldly, almost as if the author had made notes which he found no time to work-up."[2]

In view of these handicaps, it is a tribute to ecumenical scholarship that the latest versions and commentaries, Catholic as well as Protestant, should have come to general agreement about these verses. What has, in fact, triumphed is an interpretation which, to some measure, reaches back into the Middle Ages, though many modern commentators seem unaware of this. It is, moreover, an interpretation which Luther in particular championed, and which Bengel and other Lutherans furthered. It contrasted with the exegesis first attested in Augustine, followed in the glosses of the Greek, Syriac, and Latin churches alike, and continued among Catholics and Calvinists. It is only fairly recently that a common mind (at least in the West) has arisen on the matter.

It is the purpose of this essay to survey this history briefly, and then to raise the question whether a basic error in exegesis was not made from the very beginning. A new approach to our text is then offered, in the hope that this will resolve its present riddles. If I should prove right about this, the rehearsal of the history may be of value, in indicating the extent to which tradition determines exegesis both consciously and unconsciously.Even when divergences appear with their corresponding theological nuances, dividing Catholic from Protestant and Lutheran from Calvinist, as in the case of our text, the different streams may often be traced back to a common source. That is to say, one fundamental decision in the early patristic period may affect all later exegesis, and may remain unquestioned through centuries of Christian history. While we are familiar with the way in which recent methods and discoveries (such as redaction criticism at Qumran) may cast new light on the Biblical text, we should not neglect what is more obvious but perhaps less reflected upon, namely, that we tend to look at the text through the eyes of 2000 years of Christian exegesis. One commentary tends to repeat another with tedious regularity, and the glossa ordinaria is not a phenomenon purely of the 12th or 13th centuries.

The Text and Modern Versions

The correct Greek text of our passage does not present us with any serious difficulty. We may be fully content with the version given in Nestle. Later I shall have occasion to note one or two variations of it which played an important role in the exegesis. But these variants are so clearly attempts to straighten out the apparent difficulties, or to fortify the traditional interpretation, that they have no claim to being original. It is not the Greek text which is the source of the trouble: rather, it is the grammar and the meaning of the words. Here is the Greek text:

19 ἐν τούτῳ γνωσόμεθα ὅτι ἐκ τῆς ἀληθείας ἐσμέν,
καὶ ἔμπροσθεν αὐτοῦ πείσομεν τὴν καρδίαν ἡμῶν,
20 ὅτι ἐὰν καταγινώσκῃ ἡμῶν ἡ καρδία ὅτι μείζων ὁ
θεὸς τῆς καρδίας ἡμῶν καὶ γινώσκει πάντα.

Here are some modern versions representing what I might call the "ecumenical interpretation." It may be noted that The New English Bible gives this as its first variant. But only a point of grammar is at stake, and the preferred text follows the general meaning of the ecumenical consensus.

Jerusalem Bible (1966)

18 My children,
   our love is not to be just words or mere talk,
   but something real and active;
19 only by this can we be certain
   that we are children of the truth
   and be able to quieten our conscience in his presence,
20 whatever accusations it may raise against us,
   becuase God is greater than our conscience, and
   he knows everything.

Moffatt (1935)

19 Thus it is we may be sure we belong to the
   truth and reassure ourselves before Him
20 whenever our heart may condemn us;
   For God is greater than our heart and knows all.

Revised Standard Version (1946)

19 By this we shall know that we are of the truth,
   and reassure our hearts before him
20 whenever our hearts condemn us;
   for God is greater than our hearts, and he
   knows everything.

The New English Bible (1961)

19 This is how we may know that we belong to the
   realm of truth, and convince ourselves in his
   sight
20 that even if our conscience condemn us, God is
   greater than our conscience and knows all.

First variant (NEB):

and reassure ourselves in his sight in matters
when our conscience condemns us, because God is
greater than our conscience.

Rudolf Schnackenburg, Die Johannesbriefe (3rd ed.,
1965, Freiburg, p. 194)

19 Daran werden wir erkennen dass wir aus der Wahrheit sind, und so werden wir unser Herz vor ihm
beschwichtigen
20 Über alles, weswegen uns das Herz etwa verur-
teilt; denn Gott ist gesser als unser Herz und
weiss alles.

Five Basic Decisions in the History of Exegesis

To arrive at this meaning of 1 John 3.19-20,
five basic decisions have been made about the text.
Let us state them in the form of questions and look at
them in turn.

1. What is the object of καταγινώσκη in vs. 20?
2. To what does ἐν τούτῳ refer in vs. 19?
3. What does γινώσκει πάντα mean in vs. 20?
4. What does πείσομεν mean in vs. 19?
5. How should we construe the two instances of ὅτι
   in vs. 20?

1.   The first decision is the fundamental one.
Everything else turns upon it, for it gives us the central theme of the verses. The question is: what is the
object of καταγινώσκη in verse 20? Every commentator
since Clement of Alexandria[3] around 200 A.D. and Tertullian[4] between 210 and 213 A.D. has construed ἡμῶν
as the object. What the verses are all about, then, is
conscience. There are circumstances when "our heart
condemns us." καρδία stands here for συνείδησις. No
ancient or modern exegete to my knowledge has ever
questioned that. Moreover, those variations of the text
which add one or two ἡμῶν's in 3.21, so that it reads
ἐὰν ἡ καρδία ἡμῶν μὴ καταγινώσκει ἡμῶν, are clearly

34

attempts to fortify this interpretation, so that there can be no mistake about it. The Latin versions (with the exception of Augustine's) are even more explicit, not only adding nos<u>trum</u> and <u>nos</u> to verse 21, but also adding <u>nos</u> to verse 20: e.g., <u>si reprehendit nos cor nostrum</u> (Freisingen Frag. and Vulgate).

2.   The second decision concerns the reference for ἐν τούτῳ in verse 19, and is determined but not necessarily required by understanding the first part of verse 20 in terms of conscience. Almost invariably[5] commentators have referred the ἐν τούτῳ backwards rather than forwards. The earliest testimony to this is found in Augustine,[6] and it pursues its way through all the Greek and Latin glosses until it finally reaches us in Schnackenburg[7] and Bultmann[8] today. The addition of καὶ before ἐν τούτῳ in some manuscripts probably shows that it was early read in this way. That is to say, verses 19-20 are read not as providing a clue by which we may tell whether or not we are of the truth but, rather, as commenting upon our recognition of this. ἐν τούτῳ thus means: in this, namely that we do in fact love in deed and truth (v. 18), we know we are of the truth. The rest of the passage introduces the theme of conscience as a related but additional issue, which does not help us know whether we are of the truth or not, but rather follows upon our knowing it already. This backward reference of ἐν τούτῳ , as I have already observed, is not necessarily required by the conscience interpretation. Yet it is determined by it, since it yields the more acceptable sense. For John is more likely to have meant that the test whereby we know that we are of the truth lies in our loving in fact and deed, rather than in our ability to reassure an uneasy conscience,[9] or (following an interpretation to which we shall come later) to exacerbate such a conscience by thoughts of God's judgment and his all-seeing eye.

3.   The third desision concerns the sense of God's superiority in that "he knows all" (γινώσκει πάντα) in verse 20. If the first decision can be called the foundation of the ecumenical interpretation, this third decision represents, as it were, the key-stone of the

edifice. The current meaning is: "and forgives all."
God's omniscience implies his benificence; and the divine bounty extends beyond every scruple and anxiety
of conscience. As Brooke[10] puts it: "The accusations
of conscience are stilled in the presence of omniscient
holiness, which is perfect love." It is God's forgiveness, not his judgment, which is the point of the passage.

Such a rendering is in sharp contrast with the
traditional understanding of these verses, and represents a radical break with the glossa ordinaria of the
Greek no less than of the Latin Church. There the passage had been taken in a negative sense, God's greater
knowledge implying his stricter judgment. If conscience
condemns us, how much more will God!

How far back in the history of exegesis can we
trace the newer meaning by which conscience is reassured rather than alarmed by God's superior knowledge?
Since the time of Abraham Calovius (d. 1686)[11] it has
been customary to attribute this rendering to a "Thomas
Anglicus" who supposedly flourished about 1400 A.D.
Lutheran exegetes have often repeated this attribution,
the latest example being Wohlenberg in 1902.[12] The
statement, however, contains a number of confusions
which I shall try to unravel.

It is clear that Calovius derived his information from the notable Jesuit commentator, Cornelius a
Lapide (d. 1637), who wrote as follows:[13] "The exegesis
of Thomas Anglicus is forced and invalid. He says: If
great are the offences of our heart and its condemnation of us, greater is God's pity in forgiving them.
Impious is Cain's utterance: My iniquity is greater
than my deserving of forgiveness (Gen. 4.13). By 'greater' (John) means that God is more liberal, richer, fuller and more perfect than our heart, because he alone
satisfies the desires of our heart and fulfills them.
Indeed, he vastly abounds and can no more be grasped by
our hearts than the sea can be taken up in a spoon."

One might have imagined that this was a direct
citation from a medieval commentary; but it turns out
to be no such thing. Rather, it is an inaccurate summary of what Cornelius' fellow Jesuit, John of Lorin
(1559-1634) had written some twenty years earlier.[14]

Far from being what any Thomas Anglicus actually wrote, it represents a confusion of Lorinus' gloss.

By "Thomas Anglicus" both these Jesuits were referring to the author of the commentary on the Catholic Epistles which we now know to be the work of the French Dominican, Nicholas of Gorran (d. 1295),[15] but which was long attributed to Thomas Aquinas, and until more recently was bound up with his Opera Omnia.[16] As early as Sisto of Sienna, the attribution to Aquinas was suspect, and it was Sisto in his Bibliotheca Sancta who suggested[17] Thomas of Wales (d. 1340-50: i.e., Thomas Anglicus)[18] as the real author, on the supposition that scribes would readily confuse Thomas "Anglicus" with Thomas "Angelicus," i.e., Aquinas. It was thought, moreover, that the commentary cited Nicholas of Lyra (d. 1340) at 1 Peter 2.16, and for this reason an author such as Nicholas of Gorran (d. 1295) was impossible. That, however, proved a mistake, for it involved a misconstruction of the scholastic "ly" (a particle used to point to a word in a text, and here placed before quasi), which was misread as "Lyranus."[19]

Both Cornelius and Lorinus accepted Sisto's attribution, and Cornelius even mentions the (supposed) citation from Lyranus.[20] Hence we know they were referring to the commentary of Nicholas of Gorran. Nicholas' text, however, which was published under his own name in 1620,[21] does not contain the rendering of 1 John 3. 19-20 which Cornelius attributes to him. What Nicholas says, and Lorinus reports correctly, is that by the words et novit omnia, "there is noted the hope of obtaining forgiveness for those things of which conscience is remorseful. Well in his sight do we convince (our hearts), quoniam si, i.e., although our heart, that is, our conscience accuse us of any guilt that is venial, not on that account do we lose our reward: 'because God is greater etc.,' being able to cleanse our heart from its remorse and to reward it."[22]

What, then, we have in Nicholas is not an abrupt departure from the ordinary gloss as Cornelius would lead us to assume, but a cautious modification of it. Only venial sin is involved, and the traditional interpretation is given thus: "If our conscience accuses us inwardly and wishes to escape God's notice, it cannot.

. . . God will know our heart better than we, and it will be more apparent to him than to us."

The modification, however, is important, for it is clearly a step in the direction of taking the verses entirely in a consoling sense. Yet that rendering does not appear before Luther; and it is to his bold and original grappling with the passage that we really owe the full ecumenical interpretation.

Before passing to that, however, we may push back a little further than Nicholas of Gorran the tendency to modify the strictly negative sense. It seems to have arisen from a sentence which concluded the ordinary gloss: "Mighty therefore is that love which commends us to him whom we cannot evade."[23] To this Martin of Léon (d. 1221) adds: "And if he explicitly says, 'Let us love in deed, not in word,' (he does so) because, even if we from our human weakness are decieved in our love, we are not decieved in our reward, for he is greater than our heart and knows with what zeal all things are done."[24]

These passages are perhaps not entirely clear, for they conclude glosses which follow the negative interpretation. It is in Hugh of St. Cher (Hugo do Sancto Caro, d. 1263)[25] that they take on a more explicit meaning, especially so far as "being deceived" in our love goes. In glossing quoniam si reprehenderit nos, Hugh observes:"here he replies to those who might say: we are not able to love in that way (i.e., in deed, not word), because if we give to the unworthy, we fall into sin. He replies, no: not if we have a good intention in our giving. 'Because if our heart accuse us' regarding what we give to the unworthy, nevertheless it was with a good intention. 'God is greater, etc.,' that is, he sees our conscience and our intention which should be rewarded, as if he would say,'we have an evil heart and hence believe that God would not reward (merely) for a good intention; but 'God is greater than our heart,' in that he does reward our intentions." This concern about expending alms on the unworthy goes far back in Christian tradition to Didache 1.6.

We have, then, a modification of the purely negative gloss so far as intention and venial sin are concerned. How widespread this became we cannot say until

more medieval commentaries are published. Of the twenty-
eight known, only six have been printed. The absence,
however, of any reference to intention or venial sin is
worth noting in the following medieval authors: Nicholas of Lyra (d. 1340),[26] Dionysius the Carthusian (d.
1471),[27] and Jan Hus (d. 1415),[28] as well as several
commentators of the sixteenth century: Cajetan (d.
1534),[29] Tyndale (d. 1531),[30] Tittlemans (d. 1532),[31]
and Arias (d. 1588).[32] Indeed, Catholics, with few ex-
ceptions (the most notable one is the Franciscan, John
Wild, 1545),[33] came vigorously to oppose any modification, after Luther's exegesis became current.[34] This is
true of Salmeron (d. 1585),[35] Lorinus and Cornelius,
all of whom adhere to the traditional negative gloss,
while noting the rival view. Lorinus gives the facts
from Hugh and Nicholas correctly, then adds that "others"
extend the thought indefinitely to cover all sins. He
then quotes Gen. 4.13 on this connecion, a rather apt
citation in its Vulgate rendering.[36] It is this wider
view with the citation from Genesis that Cornelius,
misreading him, wrongly attributes to Nicholas, whom,
as we have seen, he calls "Thomas Anglicus."

   Such, then, is the rather confused story of
our text up to Luther, to whom we now turn. With his
exegesis there is no mere modification of the traditional gloss. Rather is there an assault upon conscience
itself; and the passage is read entirely in a consoling
sense. His lectures on 1 John were given in 1527, and
we can almost hear him thinking his interpretation out
loud in the lecture hall.[37]

   On "et novit omnia," Luther candidly observes
(as modern commentators seldom do): "Hoc verbum est apud
me obscurum. For it is not said 'he can' or 'he does'
all things. I think it is spoken of conscience, where
it is condemned or condemns, and there then happens as
in the Psalm (40.13), 'Evils without number have surrounded me . . .'"[38] Despite this hesitancy, Luther's
exposition is a vigorous defense of the view that 'novit deus' refers to God's forgiveness. "God is greater
than my heart and knows all, knows how it will turn out
for me. For he speaks of this business of conscience
which examines all secret places, freely wishes to see
the light and is trembling with fear. He says: Close

your eyes, you know nothing, you have known nothing.
'God is greater' etc. He knows peace and will grant
you rest in that condemnation of your heart. This occurs when I realize that he is greater than my sins,
which have me in their grip."[39] Or again: "Our conscience is in many respects less than our God. Against
a bad conscience you should say: You are a single droplet: God is an infinite fire which consumes you.[40]
There is no greater sin than lack of faith, 'because
they do not believe in me' (John 16.9). Only lack of
faith is without forgiveness, because it wars against
remission of sins, all of which have remission. Ex-
cellent is the saying and the sweetest promise, 'Si
nos reprehendit': for do your sins suprass the divine
bounty, are your sins greater than God's beneficence?"
"Conscience is an evil beast, because it makes a man
oppose himself." Here, we may feel, is the very heart
of the Lutheran Reformation.

By the early sixteenth century, then, the basic
decision had been made about our text. It refers to the
self-condemnation which the conscience inflicts upon us
and to the resolution of this as reflection upon God's
rich mercy and forgiveness. The translation so far
would be as follows: By this (namely by our loving in
deed and truth) we shall know that we are of the truth,
and in God's sight we will persuade our hearts (to have
thoughts appropriate to this). For (even) if our heart
condemn us, God is greater than our heart, and knows
all things (i.e., forgives all things by his greater
beneficence).

The Vulgate could be rendered that way since
both it and the Old Latin versions omitted the ὅτι before μείζων in verse 20. This, as the similar reading
in Codex Alexandrinus was clearly an attempt to smooth
out the grammar and to avoid the stumbling block of the
ὅτι before μείζων. We may further note that when this
ὅτι was read by the Greeks it was taken as resumptive,
a repetition of the preceding ὅτι and hence redundant.
Thus the 12th century scholion in Matthái: παρέλκει.[42]

4, 5.   We come now to the fourth and fifth decisions
which are responsible for the renderings with which
we started, and which we have called the ecumenical

40

interpretation. These concern the precise meaning of πείσομεν (verse 19), and the way to construe the two instances of ὅτι in verse 20. The first of these decisions was made in the early 16th century; the second I can trace no farther back than Bengel (1742)[43] and Hoogeween (1769). πείθω is translated "calm, reassure, tranquillize" (a sense it already seems to have had in the Syriac version);[44] while the ὅτι with ἐὰν is read as the equivalent of ὅ τι ἄν (whatsoever), and the ὅτι before μείζων is rendered 'because.' This brings to fulfillment the ecumenical interpretation. The 18th century could not evade the issue of the ὅτι before μείζων by merely suppressing it as did the Old Latin and the Vulgate, since it was read in the best manuscripts.

The claim that πείθω can be used absolutely in the sense of "tranquillize" our heart, set at rest the various attempts to find an unexpressed object. The ordinary gloss dependent upon Bede had supplied (persuade our hearts) "to have such thoughts as are worthy of the sight of God."[45] Nicholas of Lyra assumes, "ad verae charitatis opera,"[46] Calvin intends, "de nostra cum deo coniunctione,"[47] while Cajetan reads, "wc persuade our hearts of this very thing that we are of the truth, not by deceiving ourselves or flattering ourselves, but in the sight of God."[48]

It is possible that Augustine had anticipated this supposed sense of πείθω or rather its Latin equivalent, for he never gave an expressed object to persuademus. The two times it occurs, it is translated by Paul Agaésse "nous apaiserons notre coeur,"[49] and by H. Browne "assure our heart."[50] Erasmus says Augustine means "satisfacimus cordi nostro."[51] But perhaps Augustine's sense is not yet "reassure, tranquillize." Apart from the Syriac version, this appears first in the early Reformation, and seems to go back to Luther. While he more closely followed the literal meaning in his German New Testament of 1522 ("und bereden unser hertz fur ihm"), very soon afterwards this had become, "und können unser hertz fur ihm stillen."[52] Tyndale (1526) and Coverdale (1535) follow suit, the former reading, "and will before hym put oure hertes out of doubt," which became (1534), "and can before him quiet oure

hertes."[53] Lefèvre d'Etaples (1530) translates, "et de
ce renderons nos cueuis certains devant luy;"[54] which
may have suggested the rendering in Beza's Latin New
Testament (1565): "secura reddemus corda nostra."[55]
By the time of Abraham Calovius (d. 1686), we find:
"tranquillabimus corda nostra;"[56] and also the reference to Matt. 28.14, an error which has all too frequently been cited ever since. Finally we may mention Bengel:
"pacabimus et desistant condemnare."[57] We must, however,
note that this strained sense of πείθω was not confined
to those who followed the "ecumenical" interpretation
of our text. It equally fitted the rival or "negative"
interpretation, to which we shall come in a moment, and
which was upheld by Augustine, Beza,[58] and even the Lutheran Calovius.

The importance of the manuscript evidence in the
early 18th century had as its counterpart the more careful study of the Greek particles, which is attested by
Hoogeween's work, Doctrinae Particularum Linguae Graecae (1769). If ὅτι had to be read before μείζων, it was
possible now to construe the preceding one with ἐὰν as
the Hellenistic equivalent of ὅ τι ἄν (whatsoever),[59]
Thus the ecumenical interpretation is completed: In
this (namely by loving in deed and truth) we will know
we are of the truth, and before him (God) we will set
our hearts at rest, whatever our hearts bring against
us, because God (in his forgiveness) is greater than
our hearts, and knows (i.e., condones) all.

It was, however, a long time before this view
finally triumphed, and even now the New English Bible
is hesitant to accept both this view of ὅτι ἐάν and the
absolute use of πείθω. It prefers the other horn of the
dilemma, i.e., to follow A and the Latin by suppressing
the ὅτι before μείζων. Yet the sense remains that established in the early 16th century. However, all the
other modern versions we have cited follow Luther and
Tyndale on πείθω, and Bengel and Hoogeween on ὅτι ἐάν.

The Negative Interpretation

Before we turn from this historical survey, it
may be of interest to refer to the original interpretation which Nicholas and Hugh modified, and from which

Luther so abruptly departed, but which long survived in Catholic and Calvinist commentators. This can be called the 'negative' exegesis of verse 20, in which the superiority of God's knowledge is understood as his harsher and more alarming judgment. If our hearts condemn us, God condemns us even more. The verses then read in this way: In this (namely by our loving in deed and truth) we shall know we are of the truth, and before him (God) we shall persuade our hearts (to have right intentions). for if our heart condemn us, God is greater than our hearts and knows all things (i.e., even our secret sins, and will condemn us even more).

This interpretation is first attested in Augustine, and doubtless goes back to a yet earlier date. Augustine expresses it with a characteristic aphorism: "You hide your heart from man; hide it from God if you can!"[60] From Augustine the thought passed to Bede and thence into the glossa ordinaria, and was not fundamentally challenged until Luther. But it had a long history in both Greek and Latin churches and was championed against Luther by the Calvinists,[61] as it was continued by the Catholics until fairly recently.[62] Indeed Lutherans, themselves, were far from agreed on Luther's own exegesis; e.g., Hunnius, Calovius, Lücke and Neander[63] all rejected it; and it seems to have no distinguished exponent between Flacius (1570)[64] and Spener (1699).[65] Only with the rise of Pietism and the publication of Luther's lectures (1708) did it come into its own.

While we have no early Greek commentaries on 1 John, save that of pseudo-Didymus the Blind[66] (and he unfortunately does not gloss our verses),[67] the negative interpretation turns up in the one relevant passage in Cramer's Catena, and is repeated in pseudo-Oecumenius and Theophylact.[68] The gloss in Cramer (the foundation of which lies in the scholion in Matthäi), reads: "If, he says, we sin, we are not unobserved nor shall we escape. For if in sinning we cannot evade our own heart, but are pricked by conscience, how much more when we do anything wrong shall we fail to evade the notice of God?" The Syriac tradition is similar. Diodysius bar Salibi wrote in the 12th century: "Before we rise before him at the judgment, let us be justified.

For if we appear before our conscience to be under our own censure, how much more before God who knows all!"[69] This interpretation was, indeed, already implied by the Syriac version, which construed verse 20 as a question and rendered ἔμπροσθεν αὐτοῦ as "before he shall come."[70] Calvin's comment follows the same negative line: "He calls God greater than our heart with respect to judgment, because forsooth he sees more acutely than we, enquires more intently and judges more severely."[71]

It may well be that the battle over this interpretation,[72] which characterized the commentaries of the post-Reformation era and continued into the late 19th century, reflected the divergent theological positions of the respective antagonists. The essence of the Gospel, to Luther, lay in that gift of faith whereby the "evil beast" of conscience was finally put to rest. For the Calvinists, on the other hand, conscience played a more positive role in one's duty to recognize divine Glory. To the Catholics, who were following the traditional interpretation in East and West alike, the Lutheran view smacked too much of a Gospel without adequate moral restraints. However this may be, one of the last echoes of the Calvinist view appeared in the exposition by G. G. Findlay in the Expositor of 1905.[73] Three years earlier it had been revived by a German pastor, Wohlenberg,[74] who curiously enough seems to have been a Lutheran. Among Catholics, Camerlynck[75] still represented the traditional exegesis in 1909. Even mention of the other alternative which Salmeron, Lorinus and Cornelius had at least noted, had disappeared in Estius (1604), J. de la Haye (Biblia Maxima: 1660),[76] and Calmet (1726),[77]

Just why the newer view has come finally to triumph against the traditional interpretation has perhaps less to do with its solving more grammatical problems than its rival (for it surely does not) than with the theological spirit of the day. This wishes, and perhaps needs, more to reflect on the divine beneficence than to exacerbate consciences already too uneasy in our times of trouble. It is not insignificant that in these days of ecumenical rapprochement, Catholics are more often attracted to Luther than to Calvin. So it is with our text, though Catholics appear more prudent than Protestants in understanding the conditions under which conscience may legitimately be reassured.[78]

A New Approach

I should like now to suggest a new approach to our text. I do so with a mixture of confidence and diffidence; confidence, because I think my solution obviates many difficulties of the traditional interpretation, but diffidence, since a radical break with the glossa ordinaria is never to be undertaken lightly. I want to challenge four of the five decisions which have been made about our text, questioning the very foundation upon which both the rival views we have surveyed have rested. It was, I think, in the early patristic period that the basic error was made, and the original meaning of the verses distorted.

You will recall that by about 200 A.D. the interpretation in terms of conscience had been determined. It is attested in Clement of Alexandria and Tertullian, and, if the Christian form of the Testament of the XII Patriarchs[79] antedates them, may go back into the 2nd century. I wish to question this interpretation and to suggest that the passage has nothing to do with conscience at all. Indeed, it is precisely the error of taking ἡμῶν as the object of καταγινώσκῃ in verse 20 that is responsible for all the difficulties of grammar and translation which have been encountered ever since. It requires us to read ἐν τούτῳ backwards, instead of forwards, which is contrary to the uniform style of the Johannine letters;[80] it requires us to strain the meaning of πείθω(i.e., tranquillize, still, reassure) for which no real evidence can be cited despite the desparate attempts of so many scholars to do so;[81] it requires us to interpret God's "knowing" as his forgiving or judging, a most curious use of γινώσκει, as Luther, you will recall, was candid enough to observe; it requires us to render καρδία as the equivalent of "conscience," for which no precise parallel can be found;[82] and above all it confronts us with a theme which is most obviously out of context, so that the transition from verse 20 to 21 is made difficult. After doing the best he can with the ecumenical interpreta-

tion, Schnackenburg has to confess, "A certain harshness (in the transition) remains, but it scarcely gives
us the right to recognise a seam for distinguishing
different sources" (p. 203). The reference is, of
course, to the paste and scissors technique of Bultmann.[83] Yet we need not avail ourselves either of the
latter's radicalism or of the former's mild despair.
We can find the proper object for καταγινώσκη.

The Context

Let us look at the context. From 3.16 to 3.24,
John proposes three tests by which we may know something. Each begins with ἐν τούτῳ, and in the first
case (3.16) and the third case (3.24) the expression
is to be referred forwards. We should naturally expect
the same in our case (which is the middle one: 3.19),
especially since it is the uniform style of these letters. The first case tells us how we have known love:
"In this we have known love, namely that he laid down
his life for us." The third case tells us how we do
know the indwelling of Christ: "And in this we know
that he reamins in us, (namely) (here ἐν τούτῳ is not
picked up by any particle) by the Holy Spirit which he
has given us." The middle case (3.19) begins similarly:
"By this we shall know that we are of the truth . . ."
We should therefore suppose the author is going to pick
up ἐν τούτῳ with or without a particle, by expressing
some thought whereby we shall know whether or not we
are of the turth. He has told us how we have known what
love is: he will tell us how we recognise the indwelling. So here he should surely be telling us how to know
whether we are of the truth. That, indeed, I believe,
is what he is doing. Once we divest ourselves of the
notion that he is talking about conscience, we are in
a better position to grasp his thought, or at any rate,
to make a good guess as to what he has in mind.
Let us ask, in the light of the whole passage,
what his thought might have been. He is going, I assume,
to tell us how to know we are of the truth; and the
cardinal point in this test is to be that "God is greater than our heart and knows all things." Now, what does
that suggest? Let us take a hint from the fact that the

verses have to do with knowledge, with truth, with the
heart as the seat of understanding (its primary Hebrew
sense), with "knowing against", that is, "being prejudiced against" (the original meaning of καταγινώσκειν),
with convincing, and, later down (verse 23), with believing. Can we guess from all this what John is driving
at? Surely the point is obvious: he is going to tell us
how to know we are of the truth if we have intellectual
doubts about it, if our minds (hearts) are for one reason or another prejudiced against. Whatever heresy
he is attacking in the letter, it springs from an essential questioning of the truth because of the intellectual difficulties raised by the spirit of the times,
which has a prejudice against God's direct contact with
matter. That Jesus himself was the Christ, that the Son
came ἐν σαρκί was too much to believe. It compromised
the divine transcendence and impassibility. What,then,
is the Christian to do when he hears an "announcement"
that the man Jesus is actually the Son of God (4.15),
the fleshly incarnation of the divine? Is he to follow
his doubts and walk out of the church (2.19), or is
there another way of handling them? It is exactly this
issue which I believe John has in mind in our passage.
It is not an issue of conscience, but one of intellectual doubt; and the way it is resolved is in the recognition that our knowledge is limited in comparison with
God's. He, not we, knows all; and on the basis of the
apostolic witness we may set our minds at rest. That is
how we know we are of the truth: we accept the testimony
of the author: we do not break the bond of love in the
church; but we submit our limited understanding to God's
superior knowledge.

    If this is the thought, it admirably fits the
context both of the passage and of the letter as a
whole; and instead of introducing an extraneous digression on conscience, which requires straining both
grammar and the meaning of words beyond credibility, it
gives the words their proper and usual sense, as well
as being grammatically correct.

The Exegesis

Let us now try to render our verses in the light of this. We shall decide to refer ἐν τούτῳ forward; and we shall search for an appropriate object to πείσομεν, and to the two instances of καταγινώσκῃ (20 and 21), where no object is expressed, but is clearly understood. We shall refuse to take ἡμῶν as the object of καταγινώσκῃ, but follow Augustine's Latin text which rightly took the ἡμῶν of 3.20 with καρδία (quia si male sentiat cor nostrum). What could the object be? Nothing other than ἀλήθεια, which is what the verses are all about! It is the truth, not us, that our heart may condemn or be prejudiced against. This seems so patent that one wonders why it has not been thought of before. The early patristic exegesis has, as it were, blinded our eyes to any other possibility than rendering verse 20 as "our heart condemns us." Yet such an expression is somewhat odd, as odd, perhaps, as our saying, "our head condemns us," καρδία is seldom, if ever, the equivalent of conscience until Clement, Tertullian, and the Christianized Testament of God made it so. Unfamiliarity with the primary Hebrew sense of "heart" as the seat of understanding, and over-familiarity with the popular and semi-philosophic use of συνείδησιſ, are responsible for the error. It is Greeks and Latins who have misread John.

How, then, shall we read our text? First, does the ἐν τούτῳ refer backwards or forwards? This is a difficult question to decide. The Hebrew expression be̱zoth, like the Greek, can refer both ways, although there is only one clear instance of backward reference in the Johannine writings, i.e., John 16.30. Sometimes 1 John 2.5 and 3.10 are cited as other instances,[84] but what is noteworthy about these passages is that the ἐν τούτῳ seems to refer both backwards and forwards. It picks up the thought of the preceding sentence and then points forward to a duplication of the same theme in other words.

That structure, however, is certainly not involved in our text, and it is necessary to decide whether the reference is backwards to "loving in actuality and truth" or forwards to the resolution of intellectual doubt by the recognition of God's omniscience. Since the

other two instances of ἐν τούτῳ in our passage are
clearly to be referred forwards (3.16 and 3.24), as is
also 4.2, we should expect the same here. The difficulty lies with the construction. Can καί pick up ἐν τούτῳ?
Our author has a variety of ways of picking up ἐν τούτῳ:
with no particle at all (3.24, 4.2, 2.5-6), with ὅτι
(3.16, 4.9, 4.13) with ἵνα (4.17), with ὅταν (5.2), and
with ἐάν (2.3). There is never an instance with καί, and
while it would be tempting to read the καί in the sense
of "namely," since the καί of explanation is found in
both the Epistle (1.2) and the Gospel (1.3), such a rendering would be rash. The parallels are not sufficiently
close, and even Luke 11.34, where ὅταν is picked up by
καί in the sense of "then indeed")the equivalent of the
Hebrew gam), is not adequate evidence for our defending
the use of καί in our text as "namely."

We are thus confronted with a backward reference
to "loving in actuality and truth," in which case the
καί would be a simple copulative, or to a forward reference without a particle, in which case the καί is to be
taken as adverbial and emphasizing the ἔμπροσθεν phrase.
Both are possible, but the forward reference is what we
should normally expect in this writer. It would seem
that the mention of "loving in truth" leads the author
to the question in his mind: How can we love in truth?
What does "being of the truth" really involve? Truth
has a double sense in John: it refers both to the truth
about Jesus as the Christ come in the flesh, and also
refers to the love which flows from this right belief.
Truth is both something to be believed and something
to be done (1.6). But it is the belief which is prior.
To be of the truth (3.19) means first of all to believe
in Jesus as the Christ (2.22). This, however, is the
stumbling block. How can one believe when such a belief
contravenes the divine transcendence and impassibility?
It is exactly that problem which caused John's opponents to leave the church (2.19). That the divine should
have such a close contact with matter, that the Word
became incarnate in an actual, crucified person, was
incredible. The most these opponents were willing to
acknowledge was that Jesus was super-naturally endowed
at his baptism, but the divine effluence abandoned him
at the crucifixion (5.6-8, as Cerinthus). It is intel-

lectual doubt which stands in the way of right belief. To love in actuality and truth requires <u>believing</u> the truth, and how is that possible when the understanding rejects the belief out of hand? John's answer is clear: The human heart (understanding) lacks God's omniscience. Whatever objections the heart interposes can and must be set at rest by prayer before God himself, and by acknowledging our limited understanding. God, not we, knows all; though we ourselves can be "in the know" through the enlightenment given by the chrism of the Holy One (2.20).

Right belief, furthermore, brings confidence before God (3.21)--a theme to which our author reverts in 5.13-14. Belief in the name of the Son is the ground of this confidence, providing both an assurance of sin forgiven (2.1) and of prayer answered (3.22 and 5.15).

Our text, therefore, is one which tells us how we can know we are of the truth. The issue is raised in the author's mind by his mention of loving in truth, and it is answered by his reminding us that, whatever objections may be brought against that right belief which is essential to true love, can be resolved in prayer before God, by realising his omniscience in comparison with our own meager knowledge.

Our text will then read as follows:

> By this we shall know that we are of the
> truth, even before him (God) we shall con-
> vince our heart (of the truth), whatever
> <u>our</u> heart brings against (it), because
> <u>God</u> is greater than our heart and knows
> all things. Beloved, if our heart (as a
> result of this exercise) is not preju-
> diced against (the truth), we have con-
> fidence toward God etc.

Such a rendering is simple, plain and obvious: it fits the context perfectly, as well as the general theme of the Epistle; there are no points of grammar that cause difficulty, and no word is strained beyond its normal meaning. We take ὅτι ἐάν as the Hellenistic equivalent of ὅ τι ἄν , for which there is New Testament support elsewhere;[85] we construe it as an accusative of respect;

and we understand the order of ἡμῶν ἡ καρδία (verse 20) as perhaps a purposeful emphasis to bring out the contrast between our limited knowledge and God's omniscience.[86] Furthermore, we can see the point of the different tenses of γινώσκειν in the three tests of knowledge given in the whole pericope. We <u>have</u> known love (3.16) because, as a past event, he <u>laid</u> down his life for us. We <u>do</u> know (3.24) the indwelling now, because we have the Spirit and do not break the bond of love in the church. We <u>shall</u> know (3.19) we are of the truth, if the situation <u>shall</u> arise in the future when the spirit of the times beguiles our hearts into having prejudices against the truth; in which case we shall submit ourselves to God's superior knowledge.

Conclusion

     I think I have proposed a reading of the present text which obviates the many difficulties encountered in understanding it in terms of conscience. What it has to do with is knowledge, truth and doubt. The basic error goes back to an early patristic decision which, until now, has never been challenged. It may well be that other problems of New Testament exegesis derive from a similar set of circumstances. It is often difficult to free ourselves from the traditional tenacity of <u>glossa ordinaria</u>; and even when this was done, Nicholas of Gorran and Luther still could not free themselves completely. Their rival interpretation rested just as much upon the original error as did the view they opposed. Perhaps a knowledge of centuries of exegesis may prove, in the long run, more fruitful in helping us free ourselves from them, than the rash method of scissors and paste, which has all too long been current.

     We tend to be condemned to repeat history in proportion to our ignorance of it. It may be that the first way to begin resolving a New Testament problem is to know well the history of the exegesis. Then, to some measure, having brought to consciousness the church's long reflection on a text, we are better able to criticize it, and also to criticize our own assumptions, when we are more fully aware of the varying assumptions behind two thousand years of Christian interpretation.

51

It is my hope that this essay, in its attempt to take seriously the history of exegesis, may have some small value in pointing us in the right direction.

Cyril C. Richardson

CHRISTOLOGICAL RIGORISM AND SOTERIOLOGICAL LAXISM[1]

Students of the patristic period have often noted--sometimes with alarm--that the christological controversies in which the Fathers were engaged during the fourth and fifth centuries were not a few times marked by political maneuverings, by instances of personal bitterness and acrimony, and (less rarely than we would like to think) by outright violence. Depositions and anathemas, threats and counter-threats, injurious and even murderous plottings--these were the less celebrated companions of a process which produced a highly sophisticated and intellectually intricate series of christological affirmations and formulae. Yet, if nothing else, this observable distance between theoria and praxis in such matters indicates at least the. seriousness with which the several participants took their various positions. "What think ye of Christ?" was not a question to which one could afford to give an idle or superficial reply; too much was at stake.

Yet it would be a misperception to conclude that the many christological slogans which evolved at the time, some of them to be defended and some of them to be attacked, were of themselves of utmost doctrinal importance. Acrimony and violence aside, what surfaced as the terminological shibboleths of a particular party was but the tip of the theological iceberg. Underneath the surface was the largely unarticulated, yet much more important, conviction that the manner in which we interpret the person of Christ (christology) grows directly and intimately out of one's experience of or confidence in the "saving" work of God in and through Christ (soteriology). What was at stake, then, was not so much the victory of one party over another; of deeper concern in the christological controversies was, ultimately, if not the reality then at least the possibility of salvation. To this extent the christological controversies and debates were dead serious. If a particular formula seeking to define, for instance, the relation of the Son to the Father was seen to compromise or threaten the certain conviction as to what had been accomplished "for us and for our salvation," whether or not this conviction had been consciously articulated, it was precisely at this point that the issue was joined.

The Fathers' experience and understanding of salvation, then, were the primary determinative influences upon the emerging shape of their several christologies, an observation an increasing number of patristic scholars has been making. These influences, however, are seldom explicit in the proceedings of the councils which arrived at christological definitions. Yet they do figure rather prominently in those doctrinal expositions which attempt to argue in a sustained fashion for a specific christological viewpoint, the best known of which are, perhaps, Athanasius' De incarnatione, Gregory of Nazianzus' Theological Orations, and Gregory of Nyssa's Oratio catechetica magna. Still, those scholars who have underlined the "parasitic"[2] relation of christology to soteriology have seldom pursued the far-reaching implications of this soteriological primacy. This paper is an attempt to suggest at least some of the directions which such a pursuit might take.

* * *

The First Oecumenical Council (Nicaea, 325) inveighed against Arius' "creaturely" Christ because the participants were convinced, rightly or wrongly, that they could not be saved by a "creature." Only God could save, and therefore the Son, whom we acknowledge as Savior, must be "begotten not made"; must possess, minimally, fully divine power or, maximally, be fully divine. At the time, it was not clear whether this "full divinity" resided in the Father, per se (as the "homoousios" phrase would suggest) or in a fully divine ousia or "Godhead" in which both the Father and Son participated equally. But, if there were ambiguities in the Nicene formula, the underlying soteriological conviction was certain, and it won the day.[3] At the Second Oecumenical Council (Constantinople, 381), the "mindless" christology of Apollinaris was rejected because a majority of the Fathers believed (rightly or wrongly) that, as Gregory of Nazianzus had phrased it so epigrammatically, "quod non assumptum non sanatum." The accompanying arguments are not clear as to how extensively the Fathers in fact believed full humanity had been assumed by the Son (was it a "touching" of the human sarx or anthropos as a physician touches a wound in order to heal it, or a "coming near" to it, a "condescension" to it, a "mixture" with it, or a "dwelling" within it?). Nevertheless, the insistence that what had been "assumed" was necessarily human in the fullest sense grew out of what, on the surface at least, appeared as an unshakable soteriological principle.[4] It was out of the Arian and Apollinarian controversies, then, and out of the soteriological perceptions which informed them, that "orthodoxy" as to the meaning and significance of Jesus Christ developed. The christological confession that Jesus Christ was the eternally begotten Son of God incarnate, at once fully divine and fully human, was a definition, perhaps, as subsequent controversies indicate, which raised more question than it answered; but the soteriological foundation out of which such a definition arose is clearly visible. It is equally certain that the Fathers were anxious to insure that their christological formulations were consonant with the testimony of Scripture; continuously distrustful of "novelty," they introduced terminological and conceptual novelties by claiming that they were the formal and rational explications of what was to be found, unambiguously, in both the New and Old Testaments. Yet there is no question but that the shift from the soteriological "functionalism" of the New Testament to the christological "ontologism" of the Creeds was not wholly warranted, even by those many texts called into play to support it. Yet a deeper irony lies in this process when viewed from a slightly different perspective. A conviction as to the reality of salvation led, with increasing precision, to a definition of the "instrument" of salvation; this, in turn, issued in the assertion that one's salvation was determined by one's acceptance of the definition! Salvific efficacy was assigned, not to the event or promise of salvation (articulated initially in functional terms),

but to the "correct opinion" (orthodoxia) as to the relation of the Son to God on the one hand and to us on
the other (ontologically understood). Thus soteriological convictions were sacrificed to christological demands. While it is certain that the views of Arius and
Apollinaris (and, to a lesser extent, those of Nestorius
and Eutyches) were refuted and condemned because they
were seen as serious threats to the reality of salvation, it is certainly not clear what led the Fathers
to believe that a definition or formula could, in and
of itself, have such absolute power. A major purpose
of this paper, then, is to determine why the mode of
"orthodox" argumentation became increasingly christological (in the narrow sense) when it was the Fathers'
soteriological (in the broad sense) convictions which
were in fact being challenged.

The complexity of the problem, as well as the
irony of it, is further compounded when we realize that
the increasing precision with which christological assertions came to be formulated (what we might think of
as a kind of narrow doctrinal "rigorism") appears to
have been in direct relation to the increasing latitude
with which soteriological affirmations were expressed
(a kind of creative, open-ended doctrinal "laxism").
When the Fathers reflected upon the past "event" of salvation or upon its future "promise" (which, it is important to observe, implies some ambiguity as to its
present "reality"), their views, as well as the manner
in which they expressed those views, were diverse in
the extreme (certainly as diverse as the soteriological
affirmations to be found in the New Testament). To appreciate this diversity, one has only to think of the
proliferation of so-called "atonement theories" in the
patristic era. It becomes immediately apparent, when
we review some of these theories, that the soteriological language of the Fathers makes considerably greater
use of mythic concepts than does the christological
language of credal and conciliar dogmata. It is less
precise; it is more patient of paradox and contradiction; it is more poetic and imaginative; it has a dramatic flavor; it rejoices in ambiguity; it ignores nice
metaphysical distinctions; and, most remarkable of all,
when disassociated from the christological debates, it

is a language which avoids polemical argumentation. Soteriological models were used pluriformly, almost with abandon; never was one model pitted against another, nor did any one soteriological "doctrine" win the field against vying competitors. Never, in the patristic era, did there appear such a thing as soteriological "orthodoxy." Nor was any single articulation of salvation found so inadequate as to be seriously challenged, refuted, or condemned. Thus, there was no soteriological "heresy" either, even though some of the salvation models in circulation were certainly as theologically objectionable--some of them even more so--as some of the christological doctrines which were condemned. In a word, when the Fathers spoke of the person of Christ, they attempted to stay within the close boundaries of rational and logical thought (although this was for them, as a reading of the Chalcedonian formula indicates, an ultimately impossible limitation). But when they spoke of the work of Christ (or, more properly, of the work of God in and through Christ), their words and phrases exploded the careful boundaries of logic and entered happily into the areas of fluid imagery, of ever-changing and ever-changeable concepts, and of terminological unpredictability. On this level, at least, the soteriological language of the Fathers was faithful to the tenor of the New Testament; it was the rich variety of ways in which the New Testament authors could "name" Jesus which was lost.

When the process of christological development is viewed in this light, it is difficult to avoid the conclusion that the categories of "heresy" and "orthodoxy" must be seriously questioned, both as they were employed classically and as they have been used subsequently. The heart of the primitive kerygma spoke, simply and directly, of God's action in and through Jesus Christ. The status of Jesus was initially subsumed under the conviction that what God had done was of salvific significance, either in fact or potentially, for all people. In raising Jesus from the dead, for instance, God had declared, symbolically, the divine purpose for all of creation. The various modes and descriptions of "pre-existence," however, as well as the differing views on what came to be called the "incarna-

57

tion," while not a part of the primitive kerygma, certainly came to be viewed as implicit in it. Originally there was no univocal understanding of or insistence upon the mode of God's action in and through Christ; nor was there any one title or description or formula which claimed to exhaust the meaning of Christ. But, as we have seen, an intensity as to the reality of salvation was replaced by an ever-diminishing set of alternatives as to how one's definition of the Savior could appropriately be articulated. It was on this level that the acrimonious debates and controversies were conducted. And it was on this level--inappropriately, I believe--that the categories of "heresy" and "orthodoxy" came into full play. A penultimate concern up-staged, as it were, an ultimate conviction. An inclusive soteriological "laxism" gave way, as "heresy" and "orthodoxy" were absolutized into polar opposites, to an exclusive christological "rigorism." The affirmations enunciated in the Nicene Symbolon are a case in point. More than affirmations, they were in fact negations. Crucial to the Nicene argument were such phrases as "begotten... of the substance of the Father," "begotten not made," "consubstantial to the Father," etc. Yet such phrases were patently anti-Arian, that is, they served more to exclude Arian views than to delineate with any positive clarity those views which the Fathers sought to embrace. No wonder homoousion became more of a political battle-cry than a doctrinal assertion. The concluding paragraph of the Symbol further underlines the probability that the Fathers at.Nicaea were more sure of what they were denying than of what they were affirming:

> Those who say "there was when the Son
> was not" and "before he was begotten
> he was not" and that he came into be-
> ing out of that which does not exist,
> etc., these the holy catholic and apos-
> tolic church anathematizes.

When, after more than a hundred years of struggle, christological "orthodoxy" received its classical two-nature articulation at Chalcedon (451), the doctrinal rigorism of Nicaea had become even more pronounced:

> These things having been defined by us
> with all possible accuracy and care, the
> Holy and Oecumenical Synod hath decreed
> that it is unlawful for anyone to present,
> write, compose, devise, or teach others
> any other Creed; but that those who dare
> either to compose another Creed, or to
> bring forward or teach or deliver another
> Symbol to those wishing to turn to full
> knowledge of the truth from Paganism or
> from Judaism, or from heresy of any kind
> whatsoever--that such persons, if bishops
> or clerics, shall be deposed, the bishops
> from the episcopate and clerics from the
> clerical office, and, if monks or laics,
> they shall be anathematized.

Marcian's imperial edict of the following year (February 7, 452) gave political sanction to what at Chalcedon was already an ecclesial demand:

> Christians are to abstain from profane
> words, and cease all further discussion
> of religion, which is forbidden. This
> sin, as we believe, will be punished by
> the judgment of God; but it will also be
> restrained by the authority of the laws
> and the judges.

It is in the so-called "Athanasian Creed" that this movement towards expoliting the salvific potency of doctrine reaches its high-water mark. The Creed both opens and closes with the ultimate sanction, that is, with perdition posed as a threat to those who do not subscribe to the "truth" as formulated by the Creed. Salvation is wholly dependent, it would seem, not on one's faith as expressed but on the expression of one's faith. The very opening words of the Creed set an inexorable tone which is sustained throughout the whole of this remarkable document:

> Quicunque vult salvus esse . . . Whoever
> desires to be saved must above all things
> hold the Catholic faith. Unless one keeps
> it in its entirety, that person will sure-
> ly perish eternally.

The relation of the Son to the Father within the Triune
Godhead is carefully spelled out, concluding with what
is manifestly a soteriological codicil:

> So whoever desires to be saved should think
> thus of the Trinity.

Then comes an equally careful explication of the relation of the divine Son to the human nature assumed in
the incarnation, this time introduced by the admoni-
tion:

> It is necessary however to salvation that
> a person should also believe in the incar-
> nation.

The seriousness of the matter is further intensified
when it is claimed that correct moral behavior is as
important as correct doctrinal belief (indeed, in the
early church, the two were judged to be inseparable),
since orthopraxy, presumably, is the obvious ethical
result of orthodoxy:

> . . . those who have behaved well will go
> to eternal life and those who have behaved
> badly to eternal fire.

The Creed concludes with a final repetition of this
constant refrain:

> This is the Catholic faith. Unless one
> believes it faithfully and steadfastly,
> that person will not be able to be saved.

The pattern, then, is clear. From an inclusive
soteriological "laxism" to an exclusive christological
"rigorism"; from anathema to deposition to divine

judgment to eternal fire. From the saving efficacy of God's action in and through Jesus Christ to arrogant soteriological threats and sanctions. Is this process not even more alarming than the bitterness and acrimony which accompanied the christological debates? Is it not also a process which reveals how imperative it is to reconsider the appropriateness, Christianly speaking, of the categories of "heresy" and "orthodoxy"? As a vibrant soteriological functionalism was replaced by a static christological ontologism, it is certain that both the content as well as the implications of the primitive kerygma were manifestly undermined. The church's understanding of the significance of Jesus, both in his relation to God and in his relation to humankind, was dealt a crippling blow when christological formulae were cut off from their soterological roots and when the "power unto salvation" was seen to reside not in the love of God but in the formulae themselves. The evidence surely indicates that specific terminological formulations--at least those which were designated "orthodox"--took precedence over that awesome and ultimately indescribable experience/content to which such formulations originally sought to give testimony. The Creed itself became the object of saving belief; no longer was doctrine "transparent" to the truth because it became identified with the truth. A definition got substituted for a relationship; the "law of orthodoxy" put to flight the "spirit of freedom" which generations of Christians, before and since, have found in Christ Jesus. Such was the movement from soteriological "laxism" to christological "rigorism."

It might be tempting to construe such questions as I have been raising and such observations as I have been making as inherently or potentially detrimental to the substance of the Christian faith as it evolved during the patristic era. Such, however, is not the case, in as much as I am less concerned, in this essay, with the content of the Creeds than I am with the observable process of credal development; less with the adequacy or inadequacy of specific conciliar statements about Jesus Christ than with the use to which those statements have been put. It is not my purpose,

61

therefore, to raise questions about the homoousios doctrine of Nicaea or to challenge the "two-nature" christology of Chalcedon. Rather, it is my intent to insist that neither the homoousios formula nor the "two-nature" concept can become informative for one's understanding of Jesus Christ unless we remove from them the absolute status which the struggle between "orthodoxy" and "heresy" gave them. What follows, then, is an attempt at theological methodology, and not an attempt to discern whether this or that doctrine which has reached us from the patristic age is right or wrong. Or, to put it another way, taking my clue from the title of this volume (Disciplina Nostra), what are the implications of the movement from soteriological laxism to christological rigorism for the work of the patristic scholar today and, indeed, for the faith of every Christian?

* * *

The "content" of the Gospel of Jesus Christ, as well as the perception of who Jesus Christ is (which, as some would say, is an integral part of the Gospel), are, as the process of credal/doctrinal development patently indicates, impossible of final or verbal articulation. No words, however precise, can do justice to that which those words seek to describe or define. This is as true of the primitive confession "Jesus is Lord" as it is of the intricately woven and metaphysically profound statements of the Chalcedonian formula. All doctrinal statements are necessarily limited, tentative, and provisional; no assertion as to the meaning of Jesus Christ can capture or grasp that meaning. All we can hope for is someday to "know" even as now we "are known," someday to "grasp" the truth as even now we "are grasped" by it. If, then, the "content" of the Christian faith defies definition or accurate verbal articulation, to pose as a staunch "defender of the faith" in respect to a particular credal formulation or confessional tenet is either blasphemous or idolatrous: blasphemous to the extent that it diminishes God by pretending that God is comprehensible; idolatrous to the extent that it assigns ultimate value to something less than God, that is, to

a description or definition of God. But the alternative
to such doctrinal arrogance need not be passive agnosti-
cism or aggressive skepticism. If truth is beyond our
grasping, the diligent pursuit of truth does not thereby cease to be the constant vocation of every Christian.
To paraphrase Richard Hooker, each of us is called ever
to seek the truth, but never are we to claim to have
found it. Which is to say, neither assigning absolute
value to a relative perception of the truth, nor the
relativization of the potential absoluteness of truth
to the point that nothing can be known, is helpful for
our understanding of the Christian faith, and certainly
not helpful for our understanding, specifically, of the
significance of either the "person" or the "work" of
Jesus Christ.

1.   Which leads me to my first methodological suggestion. "Heresy" and "orthodoxy," in and of themselves,
are not necessarily out-moded or useless categories.
Short of absolutizing truth and error into irreconcilable opposites, there need to be criteria by which we
can assess the relative "rightness" or "wrongness" of
doctrinal propositions, of credal/confessional statements, and of theological assertions. The development
from soteriological laxism to christological rigorism,
traced in the first part of this paper, was possible,
I suspect, because of the unwarrented assumption that
either we can know the whole truth (e.g., about Jesus
Christ) or we can know nothing. Only such an (probably
unconscious) assumption, or something similar to it,
could have allowed "heresy" (which originally meant
"choice") and "orthodoxy" (which means "straight" as
opposed to "crooked" opinion) to be tied solely to the
content of credal formulae. Would not the liveliness of
the Christian faith have been better served had such
categories been used, rather, in respect to the intent
of such formulae? To focus, for instance, on the formal
content of the Son's "consubstantiality" to the Father
is, as we have already seen, the first step towards
separating such a statement from its experiential and
soteriological roots. To spy out the intent of such a
formula, however, is immediately to be reminded of its
soteriological context as well as of the necessarily
fluid and dialogical relation which such an assertion

has to the whole of Christian doctrine. It may be in respect to doctrinal intent, then, that the categories of
heresy and orthodoxy can find gainful employ. Heresy
and orthodoxy would thus become cooperative partners
rather than armed enemies; they would represent the two
foci of an ellipse rather than the two centers of mutually exclusive circles. Heresy would remind orthodoxy
that no specific formulation, however precise, can exhaust the content of what that formulation intends to
convey, that "creeds," in effect, must necessarily serve
as symbols, not as doctrinal ends in themselves. And
orthodoxy will remind heresy that doctrine is not the
invention of human cleverness but the faithful response
to what has already been given. Together, heresy and
orthodoxy will recognize that there may in fact be more
than one way to articulate a theological insight, and
that, whereas variety of content may on the surface
appear problematical, uniformity of intent might indeed
encourage pluriformity of content and thereby enrich
it. When "heresy" and "orthodoxy" are employed as polar
opposites, the criteria for "rightness" or "wrongness"
reside in the formulae themselves and are therefore ultimately no criteria at all. A creative, dialogical
partnership between heresy and orthodoxy, however,
will lead to the recognition of criteria exterior to
the formulae themselves and will thereby avoid further
examples of the impossible syllogistic anomaly pointed
out by Charles Raven: "God's truth is eternal; the Nicene Creed is God's truth, therefore the Nicene Creed
is eternal."[5]
2.   My first methodological suggestion, then, is
this: that we learn to distinguish doctrinal content
from doctrinal intent so that the traditional categories of heresy and orthodoxy may be freed to operate
in dialogical partnership. A second suggestion flows
directly from the first and might be stated this way:
Heresy and orthodoxy can be employed as useful categories in respect to their object (i.e., doctrinal intent), but such usefulness is directly dependent upon
the mode and purpose of their use. Relative rightness
or wrongness, that is, can be more creatively perceived
when we are sensitive and attentive to the purposes to
which a particular credal formulation is put, even apart

from the intent or content of such formulation. If, for instance, the homoousion doctrine was, as suggested earlier, added to the Nicene Symbol primarily to exclude Arian views which, for a variety of reasons (chiefly soteriological), were found wanting, then both the doctrine itself as well as the specific use (i.e., excluding, negative) to which the doctrine was put become suspect, i.e., heretical. If, on the other hand, the homoousion formula was inserted so as to suggest the possible boundaries within which the trinitarian and christological discussion might more appropriately take place, as well as to introduce a specific term which hopefully might articulate the intent of such discussion, then both the doctrine itself and the use (i.e., including, positive) to which it was put are salutary, i.e., orthodox. The criteria for such assessments, of course, are not to be found within the doctrines themselves but stem directly from our perception (never fully accurate) of the Christian Gospel, a Gospel which, at its barest minimum, proclaims positively and inclusively that Jesus Christ is the bodying-forth of God's self-giving, forgiving, creative love. My point is that the e.g., ecclesial use to which doctrinal formulae are put can in fact be judged by criteria which are not altogether arbitrary and that such ecclesial use has the immediate potential for transforming the possible rightness of a doctrinal intent into something, if not actually destructive, at least acutely ambiguous. That a doctrine can serve, as with the homoousion formula, more to exclude error that to include truth (or, perhaps, more to exclude "heretics" than to include the "orthodox") is but one example of what we might appropriately refer to as a "functional heresy." Many other examples could be given: Credal statements have been (and often continue to be) used positively or negatively, with humility or with arrogance, creatively or destructively, as gracious invitation or as coercive demand, as symbol or as idol, as affirmation or as threat, as liberating or as enslaving. The Chalcedonian formula may indeed be perceived as "orthodox" in respect both to formal content and to doctrinal intent, but such "orthodoxy" is vitiated when the ecclesial use to which it is put falls under the accusation of "functional heresy." Unquestionably such an accusation needs to be made of the movement, described earlier, from soteriological laxism to christological rigorism.

3.   That many soteriological "doctrines" existed side by side, while at the same time an increasingly narrow set of options as to christological belief were being proclaimed, leads me to a third and final suggestion in respect to the categories of heresy and orthodoxy. We have already seen that the articulations of soteriological convictions during the patristic era were (even as they are today) diverse in the extreme. Further, no one of these articulations was formally designated as "heretical" or "orthodox." Perhaps this is because it was intuitively recognized that precisely in the richness of such diversity could be found, not a diminution, but an intensification of the understanding of the reality of God's saving purposes. If, then, christological formulae were directly dependent upon their (pluriform) soteriological roots, does this not argue strongly in favor of christological pluralism as well (a pluralism, as was noted earlier, amply testified to in the New Testament)?[6] Would not a broadening of the conceptual confines within which the christological debates are conducted produce, since all attempts to describe the person as well as the work of Jesus Christ are of necessity penultimate, not a lessening or weakening of christological certainty, but an enrichment and enhancement of it, as is certainly true in the area of soteriology? I am convinced that this would be so, in spite of the fear on the part of some that it would lead to a "laissez faire" relativism or reductionism. Yet, to increase the number of legitimate models or metaphors, analogies or symbols by which we seek to interpret the significance of Jesus Christ need not lead to a "softening" of the criteria by which we assess their relative value, especially since the very relationship between a variety of models is instructive for our further understanding of any particular one of them. External criteria, as I have already indicated, are available to us, and the phenomenon of soteriological pluralism is a case in point. It is theologically significant that no one doctrine of salvation or "atonement theory" was ever

so compelling as to attain "orthodox" status; it is
equally significant that none was found to be so de-
ficient as to be condemned and its adherents anathe-
matized. Yet not all of the soteriological doctrines
or models were (are) of equal value. Judgments were
made concerning them, even if the criteria for making
such judgments were not always conscious or self-evident. Nevertheless, it is clear that, then as now,
some were more ready to use the language of justifica-
tion than the language of sacrifice,[7] some more com-
fortably disposed to models of personal relationship
than to categories of satisfaction or propitiation.
Dramatic interpretations of Christ's victory over the
demons appealed to some, while others were more concerned to see in the death of Christ God's victory
over sin and death. If the Fathers were free (as have
been subsequent generations of Christians) to explore
creatively and dialogically within the pluralistic
arena of soteriological perceptions, would it not be
equally "orthodox" to claim the same freedom for specifically christological speculations and assertions?
The criteria by which to assess what are always tentative formulations are available, but they reside neither in the formulations themselves nor in the polarization of truth and error. Again, heresy and orthodoxy,
if they are to be used creatively, must be seen to be
in dialogical relationship to each other. Only so will
the criteria for doctrinal assessment, which reside
primarily in our perception and experience of the Gospel, be brought into appropriate service.

* * *

Christian truth, articulated on no matter what
level of sophistication, cannot be bound by narrow definitions. The existence of soteriological pluralism
(laxism) in the patristic era underlines this fact and
argues for a similarly creative pluralism within other
segments of the theological panorama, expecially within the field of christology. Only if the categories
of heresy and orthodoxy are freed from the rigid confines of absolutization and allowed to operate without succombing to the temptations of what I have called

67

"functional heresy," will the creative potential for a christological pluralism be realized.

Unity was, for the early church, an almost Platonic "ideal," an ideal which suggested that, christologically, there was only one right (orthodox) way to say something. But the soteriology of the Fathers gives ample testimony to the capacity for embracing multiplicity. In spite of the saddening process from soteriological laxism to christological rigorism, there is considerable evidence in patristic writings that Christian faith, as our perception of and response to the truth of God, can be expressed, indeed needs to be expressed, more as a rich tapestry of intimate colors and shapes than as a monochrome, colorless absolute. As the lights and shadows play upon the tapestry, and as our viewpoints shift, it too will change, sometimes modestly, sometimes radically. Yet what remains the same is not the tapestry itself but its constant relationship with and abiding reference to the truth which it seeks to portray. This suggests that both the person and the work of Jesus Christ can be approached with an ever-increasing recognition of the infinitely wider boundaries within which our common discipline, disciplina nostra, as patristicists and as Christians can take place.

Donald F. Winslow

IN PRAISE OF THE KING

A RHETORICAL PATTERN IN ATHENAGORAS

For given Man, by birth, by education,
Imago Dei who forgot his station,
The self-made creature who himself unmakes,
The only creature ever made who fakes,
With no more nature in his loving smile
Than in his theories of a natural style,
What but tall tales, the luck of verbal
   playing,
Can trick his lying nature into saying
That love, or truth in any serious sense,
Like orthodoxy, is a reticence?*

The following study is appropriately dedicated to Robert Evans who encouraged its author in the development of some features of its argument. The rhetorical pattern under investigation was briefly discussed in a paper on Athenagoras delivered in a section of the American Society of Church History in December, 1971. Robert Evans served as chairman of that section and Cyril Richardson as respondent to the paper. The paper has since been published,[1] but the literary observations contained in it deserve greater attention than could be given them at that time. We welcome this opportunity to put our ideas on a firmer footing and, in so doing, to honor one who, along with Professor Richardson, raised important questions about them.

Within the first two centuries of its existence, Christianity displays a variety of responses to Roman power which range all the way from the hostile visions of the writer of the New Testament Apocalypse to the mild suggestion of Melito of Sardis (in Eusebius, H.E. 4.26.7-11) that since the Church was "nursed in the cradle of the Empire," they need not be irreconcilable enemies. Close to Melito in spirit is Athenagoras' Legatio (written somewhere between 176 and 180

69

A.D.[2]). Athenagoras does not rant (like Tatian); he is
not stubborn (like Justin); he is not simple-minded
(like Aristides). He is the best informed of the second
century apologists.[3] And he carefully stays within the
limits of the apologetic task.[4]

Yet Athenagoras' compliments to the emperors,
Marcus Aurelius and Commodus, seem so exaggerated that
they strain the modern reader's sympathy for his apologetic style. He is aware of the serious social antago-
nisms which affected the lives of Christians adversely:

> When our property is gone, their plots
> against us affect our very bodies and
> souls. They spread a host of charges of
> which there is not the slightest sugges-
> tion that we are guilty . . . (Leg. 1.4)

And he thinks that the Christians were not provided the
same legal safeguards as others (Leg. 1-2). Yet he per-
sists in believing (or pretending to believe) that the
emperors themselves are properly enlightened and need
only to be informed to set things right. He expresses
his admiration for them so extravagantly that gross
flattery seems the only possible motivation. To suggest
with Melito that the emperor and his son will flourish
if Christianity is protected along with other religions
is perhaps a reasonable argument in light of ancient
ideas concerning religion and the state; but to pin
one's hopes on an exaggerated view of imperial virtue,
as Athenagoras seems to, suggests a self-serving attitude which masks the deeper issues. Athenagoras avoids
Melito's mistake of claiming a respect for Christianity
on the part of the early emperors; but he seems to put
in its place a strained and artificial evaluation of
the philosophical character of the imperial office itself.

In this paper we shall argue that the dissatis-
faction which the modern reader feels with Athenagoras'
attitude toward the emperors is generally misplaced.
Athenagoras' position becomes more nearly intelligible
if we set his remarks in their proper context. We shall
show that his treatment of the emperors reflects standard rhetorical prescriptions for orations in praise of

the king; and we shall see that terms like "flattery" unduly narrow the function of such prescriptions in antiquity.

Our best parallels for Athenagoras' statements about the emperors are to be found in Menander's (or Pseudo-Menander's) rhetorical handbook for the writer of panegyrics.[5] It contains a chapter of recommendations "Concerning a Speech on the King,"[6] and closely related material in other sections of the manual.[7] Menander's directions for praising the king illuminate a whole stream of panegyric literature which we shall also draw on to illustrate various points. According to Volkmann,[8] panegyrics in antiquity more or less approximate Menander's model include Pliny's Panegyricus, (Pseudo-)Aristides' ninth oration ("To the King"),[9] Julian's first oration ("To the Emperor Constantius"), Libanius' fifty-ninth oration (in praise of Constantius and Constans), several of Themistius' encomia, and some of the Twelve Latin Panegyrics.[10] Menander's model continued to provide inspiration to rhetoricians to the end of Byzantium.[11] We follow Bursian in ascribing the two tractates that come down to us under the name of Menander to two different writers; and with him we date the second tractate, on which our observations are based, in the third century.[12] We assume, however, that the rhetorical tradition it represents is older. Norden thought that he found traces of it as early as Virgil's Aeneid (6.791-807).[13] Kroll rightly questions his analysis.[14] But Kroll also draws attention to a passage in Quintillian (Inst. 3.7.26-7) which shows that "the foundation for the later detailed theory was already laid"; and the closeness of Pliny's Panegyricus to the more detailed theory is sufficient warrant for our use of it in connection with our late second century apologist.

I.   One reason for the failure of previous scholars (including Geffcken) to notice the link between Athenagoras and Menander is that the former writes an apology for Christians, not a panegyric. This must be kept in mind if we are to evaluate the interrelation properly. Athenagoras' remarks on the emperors represent an adaptation of themes in praise of the king to a new form of literature for a new situation.

Athenagoras' Legatio begins with an introduction calling for just treatment of the Christians (ch. 1-2). There follows the body of the treatise (ch. 3-36). This opens with a division of topics (ch. 3) and goes on to two main lines of defence--the first against charges of "atheism" (ch. 4-30), the second against charges of immorality (ch. 31-6). The rejection of the charge of atheism takes up both the problem of theoretical atheism (ch. 4-12) and that of practical atheism (ch. 13-30). The rebuttal of the charges of immorality is relatively brief. The document ends with an appeal to the emperors (ch. 37).

Notices concerning the emperors occur in many parts of the Legatio. Especially important are the remarks contained in the introduction (ch. 1-2) and the conclusion (ch. 37). Interesting observations are also found in the treatment of theoretical atheism (ch. 4-12). Appropriately enough, these have to do with the emperor's presumed wisdom and knowledge concerning philosophical and theological matters. A few references to the emperors also occur in the treatment of practical atheism (ch. 13-30). There a criticism of pagan views of divinity is undertaken to show that refusal to participate in popular piety does not constitute atheism; this criticism makes use of analogies between divine and human kingship which, as we shall see, also throw light on our problem.

An oration modelled on Menander's prescriptions in praise of a king would take a very different form. Such an address begins with an introduction (368.1-369. 17 S; 1-6 B)[15] which usually stresses the difficulty of praising the king adequately.[16] The body of the oration (369.18-376.24 S; 7-34 B) falls into two parts: [17] the first concerns the king's native land, his family, his birth, his "nature" (physis), his upbringing and training (paideia), and his practices (369.18-372.12 S; 7-16 B).

The second part is an "account of his achievements" (372.12-376.24 S; 17-34 B). This in turn has two major foci: achievements in war (372.25-375.4 S; 19-27 B) and achievements in peace (375.5-376.24 S; 38-34 B). The "account of his achievements" is set up in terms of the four virtues. Achievements in war fall under the virtue of "courage" and to a lesser extent under "sagacity" (phronesis). Directions are given for describing military operations; and to this is appended a word concerning the king's treatment of the conquered under the rubric of "humaneness": (philanthropia) which embraces "justice" (374.25-375.4 S; 27 B). The "account concerning peace" is discussed under the headings of "justice," "sobriety," and "sagacity."

The body of the oration is followed by sections of the king's "good fortune" (376.24-31 S; 35 B), a final all-encompassing "comparison" of the king's reign with those of previous rulers (376.31-377.9 S; 36 B), and an epilogue which describes the prosperity of the "cities" and the whole empire in glowing colors (377.9-19 S; 37 B). It closes with a prayer for the success of the king's reign (377.19-30 S; 38 B).

The divergence between our two sources in form and matter is obvious; but we can still discern the rhetorical roots of Athenagoras' statements about the Roman emperors.

II.   Since the most striking parallel between our apologist and Menander is to be found in Athenagoras' conclusion, we shall begin there and then move back to the opening chapters. By that time we shall be in a position to appreciate some of the less obvious points which come out of a reading of the body of the treatise.

In Athenagoras' conclusion, the emperors (kings) are addressed as "by nature and training . . . in every way good, moderate, humane, and worthy of your royal office" (37.1). Nature and training--physis and paideia-- are closely related in Menander as we have seen (371.14-372.2 S; 14-15 B). Similar pairs of terms (physis and nomos, physis and thesis, physis and techne, physis and mathesis, etc.) occur widely in Greek literature; and the Stoic philosopher Musonius Rufus already mentions physis and paideia together in his treatise on kingship (p. 37.5-8, ed. Hense); but it is significant that this pair of terms corresponds so well to the concerns of Menander in his directions for praising the king (see also Pseudo-Aristeas, Or. 9,102d [59 (106)]). We shall have more to say about the theme of paideia presently.

For our purposes, however, the most important element in the conclusion is Athenagoras' remark concerning the prayer of Christians for the emperor and his son (37.2-3):

> We ought more justly to receive what they request than men like ourselves who pray for your reign that the succession to the kingdom may proceed from father to son as is most just and that your reign may grow and increase as all men become subject to you. This is also to our advantage that we may lead a 'quiet and peaceable life' (1 Tim. 2.2) and at the same time may willingly do all that is commanded.

This conclusion, despite a brief Biblical reminiscence, strikingly reflects Menander's advice for concluding an oration in praise of a king. There was a long tradition in Judaism and earliest Christianity of sacrificing or praying for secular rulers.[18] But the particular content of the prayers alluded to by Athenagoras has an unusual focus. We may compare Menander who, after the picture of universal peace for the cities and the empire has been painted, continues (377.19-30 S; 38 B):

> What prayers, then ought the cities to make to the Greater One [i.e., God] rather than always on behalf of the king? What better to ask of the gods than for the king to be preserved? For rains in season and produce of the sea and productivity of fruits bring us good fortune because of the king's justice. Wherefore we the cities, peoples, races, and tribes in exchange crown him, sing hymns to him, paint pictures of him; the cities are full of images, some of painted boards, others with more precious material. Then you will say a prayer requesting God that his kingdom should continue for a very long time, that it be given in succession to his

74

> children, and that it be handed on to his
> family.

Pliny similarly concludes with a prayer to the gods,
the basic concern of which is "the welfare of the emperor" (Pan. 94.2) and the birth of a successor (94.5).
It is worth mentioning here that Aelius Aristides' famous oration in praise of Rome also concludes
with a similar prayer:[19]

> Let all the gods and the children of the
> gods be invoked to grant that this empire
> and this city flourish forever and never
> cease until stones float upon the sea and
> trees cease to put forth shoots in the
> spring, and that the great governor and
> his sons be preserved and obtain blessings
> for all (109).

The connection between Aristides' Roman oration and
Athenagoras' apology has been noted by Robert M.
Grant.[20] It seems best to explain the important features they share (such as the concluding prayer) as
stemming from a common rhetorical tradition. For although (as Oliver stresses) Aristides makes indepen-
dent use of classical models, both rhetorical and
philosophical,[21] there is not doubt that there are
many "points in which the Roman oration conforms with
the rhetorical doctrine of Menander and pseudo-Menander on the proper way to praise a city."[22] And since
the praise of the city had much in common with the
praise of men,[23] we may fairly expect similar materials to appear in each.
Athenagoras' concluding remarks leave out elements smacking of pagan peity; but what he retains,
particularly the reference to the succession, strongly suggests knowledge of the rhetorical directions
for praising the king.
We return now to the first two chapters of
our apology. The salutation to the emperors as
"conquerors of Armenia and Sarmatia and, above all,
philosophers" may itself be significant. Athenagoras'
reason for writing allows him scant room for praise

75

of the king's achievements in war. Yet it is interesting to note that this is the only extant second century apology which salutes the emperors with titles that remind us of their victories, and there is no reason to suspect the authenticity of the salutation.[24] The juxtaposition of these titles with that of "philosophers" seems deliberate and may be taken (as we shall see) to echo faintly the usual practice of discussing the king's achievements both in war and peace.

The Legatio begins (1.1) with a catalogue of gods worshipped in paganism that has a double purpose: to underscore the variety of pagan gods (and consequently their untrustworthy nature); and to show the willingness of the emperors to tolerate all cults (particularly since they realize that veneration of divinity causes men to refrain from evil[25]). Then Athenagoras goes on (1.2):

> For that reason individual men, admiring (thaumazontes) your gentleness (praon) and mildness (hemeron), your peaceableness (eirenikon) and humaneness (philanthropon) towards all, enjoy equality before the law (isonomountai); the cities have an equal share in honor according to their merit; and the whole inhabited world enjoys a profound peace through your wisdom (synesis).

This is a veritable compendium of some of the most important themes found in Menander and related sources. To be sure, such themes are also found elsewhere; but their configuration in Athenagoras presupposes a view of the Roman emperors and the Roman peace that is explicable primarily in terms of the Menandrian scheme.

It is particularly Menander's directions for praising the achievements of the king in peace that are relevant here. Although Menander regards warlike deeds as taking precedence, since courage is the mark of kings (372.27-31 S; 19 B), it is true nevertheless that the king is to be proclaimed as even "more admirable" (thaumasioteros) for his achievements in peace (375.10-12 S; 29 B). In a similar vein, Pliny admires Trajan for his love of peace in spite of the fact that

he had been trained primarily for the glories of war
(Pan. 16.1). Libanius says of Constantius (after discussing his military prowess), "though he is as brilliant as this in arms, his achievements in other matters [i.e., peace] are far superior to his achievements
in arms" (Or. 59.121). In one address, Themistius an-
nounces his plan to pass over the emperor's warlike
deeds and to go on to his achievements in peace (Or.
16, 206c); and in his first oration he exalts not any
of the traditional virtues (including "courage") but
"humaneness" (philanthropia) as the special mark of
the king (Or. 1, 4b-6b). In short, Athenagoras' concentration on the achievements of the emperors in
peace not only reflects his immediate purpose but is
also in harmony with a trend that will become still
stronger in the rhetorical tradition.

According to Athenagoras' statement, the emperors' benefits devolve on individuals, cities, and the
whole inhabited world. We attend to the concern for individuals first. Menander associates the manifestation
of the king's "justice" as "mildness" (hemeron) and as
"humaneness" (philanthropia) with individual "subjects"
and "suppliants" (375.8-10 S; 28 B); the closely related term "gentleness" (praon or praotes) occurs frequently in the Menandrian tradition (e.g., Pseudo-
Aristides, Or. 9, 102d [59 (106)]; 106d [62 (111-2)];
Julian, Or. 1,16b; Themistius, Or. i, 4d, 6c; 4,
51cd; 16, 208d, 2k2c). To be sure, such language is
not confined to these orators. Isocrates held up Heracles as a model for the ideal king and characterized
him not only as sagacious and just (Philip 110) but
also as gentle and humane (Philip 114, 116). Musonius
Rufus' ideal is humane (p. 39.12-13, ed. Hense). Gentleness and humaneness are attributed to Plutarch's
prince (Ad Prince., Erud. 781a). And Dio Chrysostom
speaks of "the mild and humane king" (Or. 1.20; cf.
2.67, 2.77, 4.24). Philanthropia in particular played
a central role in the kingship ideology of the Hellenistic period.[26] But the configuration of terms with
the context provided for them in Athenagoras is more
reminiscent of Menander.

"Equality before the law" is not terminology
used by Menander; but he does join to "mildness in

justice" and "humaneness" praise of the king as "easy
to approach" (375.8-10 S; 28 B) which suggests respons-
iveness to individuals in the adjustment of complaints.
We shall have more to say about this important theme
later. Meanwhile we may note that Menander presently
advises the orator to praise the beneficial effects of
the administration of justice and among other things
remarks on the just governors sent out to "peoples,
races, and cities" as "guardians of the law" who are
"worthy of the king's justice" (375.18-21 S; 30 B; cf.
Libanius, Or. 59.163). Such justice is illuminated in
Menander's directions "Concerning a Public Address"
(to a ruler) where many of the same themes are sounded;
here he brings out one aspect of equality before the
law when he says that the ruler is above bribery and
"does not honor the wealthy before the powerless" (416.
5-10 S; 6 B). It is also worth noting that the ideal
of equality before the law plays an explicit and important role in Aelius Aristides' Roman Oration precisely in a passage in which the equal treatment of
the weak and powerful figures significantly (38-9).27

Before passing on, we may observe that later
in the introduction, Athenagoras adds a point to his
description of the emperor's impartiality that is relevant here. Because of the emperor's wisdom (2.3):

> those who are defendants before you do not
> lose heart though accused of the greatest
> crimes; and since they know that you will
> examine their conduct and not pay atten-
> tion to meaningless labels or to false
> charges from the prosecution, they are
> equally disposed to grant the justice of
> a favorable or unfavorable decision.

The middle section of the statement reflects the immediate situation; but it is framed by a sentiment of
more general applicability. This sentiment finds a
good parallel in Pseudo-Aristides. The king's justice
(we are told) is exact but correctly leavened with
philanthropia:

> In any event, there is no one who leaves

not having gained justice; nor yet does
either a plaintiff when he has lost his
case or a defendant when he has been con-
victed find fault with the judgment; but
both, acquiescing and making obeisance,
go away; <u>and</u> <u>both</u> <u>he</u> <u>who</u> <u>has</u> <u>lost</u> <u>his</u> <u>case</u>
<u>and</u> <u>he</u> <u>who</u> <u>won</u> <u>his</u> <u>case</u> <u>agree</u> <u>about</u> <u>what</u>
<u>has</u> <u>been</u> <u>determined</u> . . . (9, 104d)

The passage is unusual in our literature but has all
the appearances of a commonplace. The parallel shows
that the extravagance of Athenagoras' remark is not
unique.

When Athenagoras thinks of imperial benefits,
however, he thinks not only of individuals but also
of cities. The theme is emphatic in the statement under discussion and is repeated in the next section:
"The whole world has enjoyed your benefactions both
as individuals and as cities" (2.1). Athenagoras, in
fact, is strongly oriented to the "cities" of the empire: the cities are honored by the emperors (1.2);
they enjoy their benefits (2.1); Christians are accused of "not recognizing the same gods as do the cities"
(13.1; 14.1); if Christians are atheists so are "all
cities and all peoples" (14.2); in some "places, cities, and peoples" there are idols that have magical
power (23.2).

This orientation to the cities of the empire
has much in common with the rhetorical tradition upon
which we have drawn. One of the most interesting observations of Oliver in his discussion of the Roman
Oration is that "Aristides thought of the empire as
a league of cities."[28] As he explains more fully,
"the idea of Rome is made to fit into a traditional
mould of international organization, approved by
Greeks."[29] And again, "educated Greeks of the second
century after Christ thought far more of an ideal
league of free cities under the hegemony of one polis,
and it is particularly in this perspective that Aristides, with deliberate reminders of Isocrates, would
place the international organization created by Rome."[30]
A similar orientation characterized Menander and the
Greek panegyrists in the same tradition (Pliny reflects

a more Latin conception of the relation between Rome and her "provinces"). According to Menander, we are to say that the emperor sends out just rulers to "peoples, races, and cities" (375.19 S; 30 B). In the epilogue we are to comment especially on the "blessings of the cities" and in such a way that their good fortune is seen to depend on the peace of the empire; for we are to say that "the market places are full of wares, the cities are full of feast and festivals, the earth is cultivated with peace, the sea is sailed without danger, piety concerned with the divinity increases, honors are distributed to each in a way that befits it, we do not fear barbarians, we do not fear enemies," and so forth. The "cities, peoples, races, and tribes" give honor to the king in return for all his favors (377.10-28 S; 37-8 B). The theme is impressively developed by orators in the Menandrian tradition (see Pseudo-Aristides, Or. 9,111d [66 (119)], "the whole land is at rest . . ."; Libanius, Or. 59.171, "the land is one, the sea is one . . ."; Themistius, Or. 16, 212ab; Pan. Lat. iii [5], 15), although it also has old roots in Roman imperial ideology.[31]

It is this sort of thing that best explains Athenagoras' remarks about the "profound peace" of the empire and the honors accorded the "cities" (1.2). It is interesting to observe that when Athenagoras moves beyond "cities" to "peoples" (ethne), the terminology is in line with Menander's own references to "peoples" (ethne) and "races" (gene) as well as "cities." More striking is the parallelism between Athenagoras' statement that "the cities have an equal share in honor according to their merit" (1.2) and Menander's remark, prescribed for the epilogue, that "honors are distributed to each in a way that befits it" (377.14-15 S; 37 B). "To each" (hekastois) in Menander seems to refer to collectivities--that is, the cities--as the context indicates (see the more complete quotation in our preceding paragraph) and as the plural form suggests (as Liddell and Scott note, s.v., hekastos in the plural may indicate "all and each severally" or "each of two or more groups or parties"). Athenagoras' comment has the appearance of a slightly rewritten directive of the type given by Menander.

In a Menandrian epilogue, the peace of the empire is linked closely with strength of arms by which the emperor effects it (377.15-19 S; 37 B). It is hard to believe that Athenagoras was not aware of this (we may recall that Christians pray that the emperors' "reign may grow and increase as all men become subject" to them; 37.2); and this background may explain the unusual salutation of the emperors as conquerors of the Armenians and Sarmatians (we may recall, too, that, according to Menander, "we do not fear the barbarians"). In any event, all such benefits are brought about, according to Athenagoras, by the emperors' "wisdom" (synesis). The term is used by Menander as a variant for "sagacity" (phronesis)--the virtue by which the works of peace are accomplished (376.18 S; 34 B), although it is also relevant for success in war (373.1-17 S; 20-1 B).

So much for our exposition of the first compendious statement of Menandrian themes by Athenagoras. Variations occur in other parts of the introduction. The kings are "great and most humane and most fond of learning"; consequently they are expected to stop the abuse of Christians "by a law" just as the whole world "both as individuals and as cities" has enjoyed their benefactions (2.1). They have a "reputation for justice" which they should seek to preserve (2.2). Men can expect equitable treatment from them no matter how serious the crime with which they are charged (2.3). To the parallels from Menander given above we need add only one: that the king gives just laws, cancelling the bad and promulgating the good (375.25-6 S; 31 B; cf. 373.13 S; 21 B). It is interesting that in this connection Menander mentions the salutary effect of good lawgiving first of all on the stability of marriage (375.27 S; 31 B)--a theme not neglected by others in the same tradition (e.g., Julian, Or. 1, 46d-47a). It is probably no accident, then, that in rebuffing charges of sexual immorality, as he does later, Athenagoras refers to the "laws" established by the emperors and their ancestors "to further every form of justice" (34.3).

Another major theme is sounded in the introduction: the emperors are "most fond of learning" (philomathes, 2.1). They can be trusted to understand Athenagoras because of their "philosophy" and their "training" (paideia, 2.3). "Love of learning" and "love of truth" can be expected of them (2.6).

This emphasis on philosophical competence, as we have seen, appears initially in the salutation. It fits well with Athenagoras' desire to picture Christianity as possessing a pure (philosophical) theism which superior minds--such as those of the emperors-- can recognize as the very antithesis of atheism. But the theme also reflects the requirements of Menandrian panegyric. Normally one is to speak of the king's upbringing; but if it was not noble (and Marcus Aurelius, though his ancestors for three generations held high offices of state, was an adopted son of Antoninus Pius), one is to discuss his paideia (371.23-23 S; 15 B). In any event, the latter suited Athenagoras' purpose better, and in close connection with it he went on to credit the emperors with some of the same gifts noted by Menander in considering the nature of the king's soul: "love of learning (philomatheia), quickness, eagerness about studies, his easy grasp of what is taught" (371.25-29 S; 15 B). Especially important is Menander's next remark: "if he is a man of letters, you shall praise his philosophy and his knowledge of letters" (371.29-30 S; 15 B).[33]

Not many of our panegyrists had the opportunity to exploit this possiblity. Yet from the earliest period efforts were made to appropriate the theme. In discussing Trajan's accomplishment in peace, Pliny praises the emperor for his constant attention to rhetoric and philosophy: "you discharge whatever they enjoin, and you love them as much as you are approved by them" (Pan. 47.2). The high point of the development comes in Themistius where Plato's idea of the philosopher-king is elaborated at great length (e.g., Or. 2, 29d-34d). This is not to say that for Themistius the emperor himself was in fact a philosopher. The point is that he embodied all the virtues of philosophy whereas admiring philosophers (like Themistius) articulated them.[34] Athenagoras, then, is responsive to an impluse in the rhetorical tradition that will become even more important. And since Marcus Aurelius

(though certainly not his son Commodus) was a philosopher, Athenagoras had all the more reason for pressing
the point. But Athenagoras knows nothing about Marcus
Aurelius' philosophy as such. His view of the emperor
is drawn from the stock themes of rhetoric.

A number of items scattered throughout the
body of the treatise also suggest the influence of
the rhetorical tradition. The emperors should recognize true theology, remarks Athenagoras, since they
"surpass others in wisdom and reverence for the truly
divine" (7.3). Menander tells us that whether the king
was trained in letters or arms we are to say "that he
manifestly excels his contemporaries in the things in
which he was trained" (epaideueto; 371.29-372.1 S; 15
B). An extreme form of such praise occurs when Athenagoras asserts that the emperors are superior to all
men over the whole range of paideia, excelling all the
specialists in all the branches of learning (6.2)!
Athenagoras will even credit them with knowledge of
the Hebrew prophets (9.1)! But such praise was also
traditional in orations on famous people. It occurs
in Gregory of Nazianzus' encomium of Basil (Or. 43.23);
and what is even more important for our purposes, something very much like it appears in Pseudo-Aristides
(9,102d [59 (106)]):

> For having learned what should be learned
> and having been trained and having neglect-
> ed no good thing, nor yet being untutored,
> but having ordered his soul by all the
> branches of virtue, it was only to be ex-
> pected that he would avoid failure . . .

By nature and training he gained a share in all the
best things, "not in a moderate degree, not yet as
any others, but far beyond each."

The greatness of the emperors is such that it
provides a fitting analogy in Athenagoras to the
greatness of God. From them one can learn not to wor-
ship the world rather than its maker. For when the
emperors' subjects come to them, they do not neglect
their rulers in order to admire the beauty of the imperial residence; similarly, "not the world but its

Maker ought to be worshipped" (16.1). It is the emperors, not the residence, "from whom they also would receive what they request" (deointo; 16.2). Another reference to gaining "requests" (deontai) from the emperors will appear in the conclusion to the Legatio (37.2).

Here we must pause to comment on the picture of the emperors as open to all men who come to them to have their requests fulfilled. For Menander is also concerned about the king as one who pays close attention to the affairs of his subjects. As we have already observed, Menander notes "their gentleness in justice to their subjects, their humaneness to those who make requests (deomenois), (and) their accessibility" (375. 8-10 S; 28 B).[35] The theme is an important one in the related rhetorical tradition. Pliny (Pan. 47.3-6), Pseudo-Aristides (Or. 9,106d [62.63 (112)]), Libanius (Or, 59.122), and one of the Latin panegyrists (Pan. Lat., xii [2], 21) all stress the emperor's accessibility and occasionally develop it impressively.

Some difficulties are felt in dealing with it: First, whereas Pliny seems to have the upper classes in mind (and this no doubt was closer to reality), others suggest a greater openness. Pseudo-Aristides, for example, discusses the theme in connection with the emperor's humaneness "to the whole citizenry" and indicates that he is like the king of all (God) in responding "to all those who make requests" (hapasin tois deomenois). Second, in Pliny's day, it was possible for the orator to join an emphasis of the emperor's accessibility to an equal emphasis on the quiet and reverent atmosphere that characterized the imperial residence; the later Latin panegyrist, on the other hand, explicitly contrasts the openness of Theodosius to all men with the secretive nature of some of his predecessors who refused to let the quiet and sanctity of the royal palace to be disturbed by free access. In any event, it is interesting to note how the theme of accessibility and the emphasis on approaching the emperor in his residence converge; a similar convergence is evident also in Athenagoras.

This convergence may explain the ease with which Athenagoras moves his comparison between God

ruling his beautiful world and the emperor dwelling in
his beautiful residence. To be sure, he is careful to
qualify the comparison: "now you as emperors adorn imperial lodgings for yourself, but the world did not
come into being because God needed it" (16.2). Yet
Athenagoras speaks not only of the beauty of the royal
residence but also of its "august" character (to sem-
non), a term which has many associations with things
divine. His comparison, then, may well have been suggested by the tendency, noted as early as Pliny, not
only to compare God and the emperor (Pan. 1.3), but
also to speak of the royal residence as a kind of sanctuary (Pan. 47.5-6). Menander is also familiar with the
idea. After dealing with the achievements of kings in
peace (that is, achievements having to do with mildness, humaneness, and accessibility), he advises us to
add the following: "they (the kings) save the sick man
like the sons of Asclepius, and just as those who flee
to the inviolate temple-grounds of the Greater One
(God) can gain relief--for we do not try to drag anyone away--so the king frees from sufferings" those who
come to him (375.13-18 S; 29 B).
    The way in which the comparison is turned in
the first oration of Themistius (1a-3a) is even more
striking for our purposes and in spite of its late date
deserves mention. Themistius claims that the man who
understands the king's soul is able to admire the king
himself rather than the things that are his. He says
it is like being able to get beyond the fine exterior
of a temple to the shrine itself. Or if you need a
still clearer analogy (he says), it is like being able
to get beyond God's works (sun, moon, stars, and the
heaven) to God himself! Perhaps the passage was sharpened by exposure to Christian theology, but Themistius'
mind is fundamentally pagan, and it is fascinating to
see how it moves along paths so much like those previously taken by Athenagoras.
    These comparisons are worked out in a variety
of ways, and it is hard to be sure that they have a
great deal in common. But they breathe the same atmosphere and evoke similar images of the imperial residence and the royal personage within.
    That we are on the right track gains support

from another passage in which an even more daring analogy is involved (18.2):

> May you find it possible to examine by
> your own efforts also the heavenly king-
> dom; for as all things have been subject-
> ed to you, a father and a son, who have
> received your kingdom from above (anothen)--
> "for the king's life is in God's hand"
> (Prov. 21.1)--so all things are subordi-
> nated to the one God and the Word that is-
> sues from him whom we consider the insepar-
> able son.

Here Athenagoras is exploiting the special situation
presented by the co-rulership of the empire. But his
theory of the divine right of kings is one that repeats, in a restrained manner, rhetorical motifs. For
according to Menander we are to say (if we have nothing to say about their family) that kings "are sent
from God and are truly emanations (aporroiai) of the
Greater One;" like Heracles, the king may appear to
be born of men but "in fact has his nativity from
heaven (ouranothen)" (370.21-26 S; 11B). Again, it
is remarkable how Athenagoras' analogy, ad hoc as it
seems to be, anticipates later developments. Particularly important is Eusebius' application of Binatarian
theology to the politics of the Christian court (De
laud. Const. 3.4-6; PG 20, 1329a-1332a). And, as
Straub has pointed out, there is something very much
like it in one of the Latin Panegyrics.[36] Athenagoras
exploits the situation in a way that reflects the
deepest rhetorical instincts of antiquity.
      A more definite link with pagan ideology is
provided by the word anothen, "from above," used in
this connection. It is reminiscent of Menander's ouranothen, "from heaven"; and it has an exact parallel
in his chapter "Concerning a Speech on the Crown"
(bestowed on a king): if the king's family cannot be
made the basis of praise, we are to say that "God
pitied the human race from above (anothen)" and so
brought about the king's birth (422.16-19 S; 2 B).
To judge from Themistius, who makes full use of the

term, it lived on in the minds of many rhetoricians.
Themistius argues, for example that Constantius received signs of divine providence "from above" in that
he effected a consolidation of the kingship without
bloodshed (Or. 2, 38b-39a; cf. 46bc); he says that
Gratian was called by God and proclaimed the decree
which is "from abuve" when he rescued the empire from
all its woes (Or. 16, 207b); and philosophy, according
to a passage which catches up some of the most grandi-
ose themes of ancient royal ideology, declares that
the king (Jovian) is a "living law . . ., a divine Law
coming down from above (anothen) in time, from the
Eternal Good, an Emanation (aporroen) of that Nature,
a Providence nearer the earth," and so forth (Or. 5,
64b).

A useful summary of Athenagoras' indebtedness
to the Menandrian model is provided in his introduction where Christians are described as "the most pious
(eusebestata) and righteous of all men in matters that
concern both the divine (to theion) and your kingdom
(basileia)" (1.3). This sentiment is reminiscent of
one of Menander's alternatives for introducing a speech
in praise of the king: we may say "that the two most
important things in the life of men are piety (eusebia)
concerning the divine (to theion) and boldness[37] concerning the king (basilea)" (368.17-20 S; 3 B). Our
apologist is prepared to model the life of Christians
on pagan ideal canonized by the rhetoricians.

III.   The historical question is whether this literary relation reveals an ideological affinity that is
more than skin deep. Two questions may be distinguished. First, does Athenagoras' neglect of many of the
rhetorical themes show that there is a deeper cleavage
than may appear on the surface? Second, how seriously
are any of the themes to be taken (whether in Christian
or pagan writers) as reflections of significant social
and political values in the Roman Empire?

Both questions are difficult to answer. Concerning the first, we must give liberal allowance for
the differences between the literary genres involved.
Nevertheless, a few obvious points may be made. Athenagoras underscores the essential agreement between

the theism of Christians and that of sophisticated pagans (6.1-4); yet he cannot hide the fact that his monotheism is more radical than theirs, since his makes no room for popular religion (13-30). We should expect, then, that the tendency of rhetoricians to attribute a kind of divinity to the emperors would also be avoided.

A glance at the themes which we have reviewed suggests that this is so. Athenagoras knows that the emperors gain their authority "from above," as we have seen, and that (as Menander would put it) they are "sent by God" (370.22 S; 11 B). But he avoids any suggestion of a metaphysical descent from God. Whereas Menander regards kings as "emanations" from God, Athenagoras confines that term to God's Spirit (10.4; 24.2). Athenagoras is loyal but not worshipful.

It is also significant that Athenagoras subordinates so severely (if not entirely eliminates) the theme of the emperors' achievements in war. They are praiseworthy "above all" because they are philosophers. They are just, they are humane, they are sagacious. But the virtue of "courage"--that special mark of kings according to Menander--is missing. We have suggested above that Athenagoras faintly echoes the rhetorical interest in the emperors' campaigns; but even so, he can do nothing significant with it in defense of the cause of the Christians.

In the end, Athenagoras' view, derived from the Bible, that the king is in God's hands checks the most extravagant claims of the rhetoricians and sets a limit to imperial power. The emperors' task is to provide a framework within which all men, including Christians, can pursue their lives in peace and quiet.

But the unwillingness to pursue these ideas further and the readiness to adopt to much of the pagan imperial ideology intact explains why after the conversion of Constantine, Christian emperors could continue to function in ways appropriate to divine beings.[38] Athenagoras' _Legatio_ is a valuable witness to the manner in which the Christian élite was unconciously preparing the church for its role as the major vehicle of religious values in the Roman state.

The importance of Athenagoras in this respect has not been sufficiently recognized because the link

with the rhetorical tradition in this connection has
not been understood, but also because that tradition
has itself been misunderstood. The panegyrics have
been dismissed as bad literature and interesting only
for the historical facts buried in them. In particular,
they have been viewed as "flattery" indulged in by de-
cadent litterati in search of imperial favors.[39]

It has become increasingly clear, however, that
this characteristic of our literature is inadequate.
Straub in particular has emphasized the "publicistic
significance of the panegyric literature."[40] These addresses were not gross flattery for personal ends as
Schanz and Geffcken thought, but played an important
role as an ancient form of public relations. No emper-
or, Straub insists, simply rewarded flattery with a
position in the imperial government. Rather, the abilities of the rhetorician were probed, and a resulting
appointment, such as that of magister memoriae, had a
wider purpose than providing for sycophants.[41]

In this connection, Straub comments at length
on Menander and the apparent extravagance of his directions for praising the king.[42] To be sure, Menander
advises the rhetorician to invent something about the
divine birth of the king if his family background proves
undistinguished (371.3-14 S; 13 B). But that (according
to Straub) is not "frivolous." The rhetorician did not
expect his traditional mythological comparisons to be
taken literally; yet he would have agreed with the philosophers that the emperor was somehow closer to the
divine than other men. He attributed to the emperors
what the emperors had long claimed for themselves;
and no inner rejection of these claims lay behind the
conventional phraseology. In short, these ideals of
kingship were taken seriously by all.

Straub also devotes special attention to Themistius and credits him with a genuine sense of philosophical mission to the emperors under whom he served,[43]
The philosopher (Themistius) brings to expression what
the king, as the image of God, instinctively knows and
does. But the articulation of the imperial ideal also
serves as an appeal to the emperor to become what he
is. However far from reality the rhetorical picture
of the emperor may have been, the ideal could never

be totally ignored, and they provided the atmosphere that made it even conceivable that the emperor would take an interest in the "requests" put to him. Understood in light of these developments, Athenagoras' praise of Marcus Aurelius and Commodus loses much of its strangeness.

It is also possible, of course, to evaluate these materials from outside the context of the society which produced them. Starr, who is fully alert to the publicistic significance of the panegyrics, sees them as the furthering of "the acceptance of absolutism."[44] In the study referred to at the beginning of this paper, we criticized such "imperial theology" as insufficiently realistic from the standpoint of a more or less Augustinian view of man and society.[45] Even Oliver, who insists that Aelius Aristides in his praise of Rome "could not have dilated so long on non-existent virtues,"[46] grants that "the historical and political judgments of Aristides are very superficial" and that he spoke not as "an average provincial or even an average Greek" but as a member of the favored class.[47]

These political, social, and theological judgments on our literature are legitimate in terms of their own frames of reference. But they are not necessarily as significant when seen against the background of what was possible and comprehensible in the Roman Empire itself. With that in mind, Athenagoras' praise of the emperors may be seen as a sensitive response to an important strand in ancient political thought and a remarkable anticipation of the flowering of these ideas in the fourth century.

William R. Schoedel

MARCION'S JEALOUS GOD

I.   After A. von Harnack's[1] brilliant monograph it became imperative to readdress the question of Marcion's relationship to gnosticism. Harnack, except for a footnote,[2] magnified Marcion's originality and denied almost any relationship to gnosticism so that Marcion was no longer positively related to the history of the early second century; according to Harnack, Marcion rediscovered the radical prolcamation of the Apostle Paul in the face of the all-pervasive so-called early Catholicism. Such a verdict, however, contradicted the testimony of the Church Fathers, especially Origen, if, for a moment, we set aside the heresiologies of Justin Martyr and Irenaeus. Contributions, reemphasizing Marcion's ties to gnosticism, have been made by U. Bianchi,[3] F. M. Braun,[4] and recently B. Aland.[5] It has been recognized in all these studies that Marcion's teachings cannot be deduced from his reading of the Bible alone but that he presupposes gnostic themes and concepts and takes over, or rather lets transpire, some of them. Nobody, however, wants to deny Marcion's originality. Yet, Bianchi identifies the following gnostic topics in Marcion: (1) the subject of knowledge; (2) a reflection of the gnostic spirit-matter dualism in (a) a separate creation of the unknown God in contrast to the material creation of the creator, and (b) the disdain of the flesh whereas souls are saved, and (c) Marcion's docetism in which the exceptional position of the human soul gives reason for surprise and in which matter plays a subordinate role but remains the presupposition for the contrast between the two gods radicalized by Marcion. The major difference from gnosticism, according to Bianchi, is Marcion's denial of a divine <u>pneuma</u> in man. B. Aland concentrates on three characteristics exhibiting Marcion's relationship to gnosticism: (1) the self-designation of the creator god by "I am God and nobody besides me" (<u>Isa</u>. 45.2); (2) salvation from this world, and (3) the reverse evaluation of the Old Testament. In contrast to gnosticism, Marcion takes the otherness of the unknown god seriously; the major consequence of this is to be seen in his anthropology making man completely a creature of the creator and thus not claiming the salvation of a non-worldly element in man. Such a radicalization leads to the dismissal of cosmogony because it was the objective of gnostic cosmogonic myths to show the presupposition of salvation, namely, the presence of a non-worldly element in man. Aland (p. 442) elaborates what Bianchi had already indicated: The human soul is to be saved; yet such an idea lifts the human soul beyond the sphere of the creator. The implicit contradiction, Aland explains, has to be recognized as an anti-gnostic assertion; it is Ipelles who corrected his master at exactly this point and asserted that the soul has a heavenly origin. To sum up Aland's argument about the apparent contradiction in Marcion: If man as a whole is a creature of the creator god, then there is no reason why it is the soul alone which is capable of salvation, the body having also been made by the creator.

What does all this mean? Nobody will deny that Marcion conceived his own teachings through the impact of his reading of the apostle Paul. But it is imperative to recognize for which kind of criticism or reformation of gnostic doctrines the apostle enabled him, if it might be assumed that Marcion is to be understood on a gnostic background. One may evaluate Marcion's interpretation of Paul favorably or unfavorably; yet, it is a rewarding task to account very precisely for the aspect of Paul's proclamation which appeared to be decisive for Marcion in his particular situation. Not only a valuable contribution to the understanding of Paul will result from such an account, but also a contribution to some central questions of Christian theology. Aland indicates (pp. 420-22) that such contrary orientations such as Harnack's "liberal theology" as well as Barth's "dialectical theology" have appealed to a Marcionite interpretation of Paul, the latter obviously without naming Marcion. Harnack begins his study with a definition of religion in order to demonstrate that Marcion fits all conditions of religion as such. True religion is paradoxical, unambiguous, and exclusive, i.e., paradoxical because it is free grace beyond reasoning, unambiguous because it rejects syn-

cretism, and exclusive because it is focussed on salvation alone. Harnack summarizes (p. 33): "It results
from this that the hostile sphere from which salvation
through Christ sets free can be nothing less than the
world, including its creator." At the end of his book,
however, he asks the question: "Is it not a false in-
teriority, even lack of concern, if the whole world is
to be given up because it cannot be saved, if one is to
focus solely on the proclamation of the gospel and to
attempt no action at all? Does not all action presup-
pose the reformability of reality and, thus, its original goodness?" (p. 234) One could furnish parallels
from Barth to these last critical questions which indicate both his closeness to and distance from Harnack.
In the preface to the second edition of his Epistle to
Romans, Barth acknowledges that Harnack's Marcion per-
plexed him, although he says that an elaboration of the
crucial differences is not necessary. I mention all of
this because it shows that an acquaintance with Marcion
might improve the precision of a theological interpretation of the apostle Paul.

II.   Marcion distinguished between a lesser creator
God and a greater unknown god. According to all reli-
able sources, he understood the contrasting distinction
between the two gods to be the contrast between "just"
and "good."
        Harnack has brought up a problem, however,
which must be clarified before I attempt to explain
Marcion's distinction between just and good. To be sure,
all sources agree that the distinction between just and
good is an exclusive one for Marcion. Harnack, however,
claims that Marcion did not reject the last and justice
in an absolute way but only the justice of the creator;
he states in italics: "One has to conclude that, according to Marcion, both gods are in agreement in that they
declare evil to be evil and love of God and neighbor to
be good." "Justice is only rejected in the way the creator exercises it" (p. 111). Aland (p. 425) is right in
concluding that Harnack softens the contrast between
just and good or law and gospel through such assertions
and that, in addition, he distorts Marcion's intentions.
Yet, Aland believes with Harnack that Marcion's termi-

nology is ambiguous and that, in fact, the law is
called good. Aland suggests a solution which would
preserve the otherness and strangeness of the good
god despite this terminological ambiguity. She wants
to recognize in Marcion's wording a necessary device
for expressing the essential otherness of the unknown
god. "There is principally no mode of human speech to
describe this god appropriately." "If, therefore, Marcion calls the strange god 'good' and recognizes his
proper nature in 'goodness,' then it is self-evident
that such goodness is something totally and principally different from everything termed 'goodness' in
the human sphere. But since there existed no other
more proper term, Marcion was forced to use this one."
Marcion, she continues, could not dispense with the
words 'good' and 'goodness.' "Marcion was by no means
a libertinist. Therefore it is natural that he acknowledges the law, i.e., the moral law, to be holy and
also true (cf. Rom. 2.20). Yet, such being good and
holy and true has nothing whatsoever to do with that
god and asserts nothing at all about him" (p. 426).

A question arises: where are the testimonies
supporting the assumption of an ambiguous terminology?
The answer to this question will determine what Marcion
understood by law and justice. It is only a detailed
analysis which can provide the material basis for an
appropriate understanding of Marcion.

At first, it sould be noted that Harnack does
rely on nothing else but Bible passages supposedly retained by Marcion and not eliminated by him. When H.
von Soden reviewed Harnack's study, he asked already
the question as to what gives us the right to isolate
such passages and to interpret them contrary to Marcion's explicit statements because Marcion himself
must have recognized the contradiction.[6]

Harnack begins with the correct insight that
the essential quality of the creator god is justice
(p. 99). Then, under seven points, he lists the ways
which exhibit the malitia of the creator (p. 100).
Badness and justice coincide, according to Harnack,
because it is the justice, or rather the order, of a
despot. Despite all his badness, "this god wants to be
just, and he is just as long as his honour is not

96

jeopardized and his limitness not exhibited. Therefore, his activity is not badness but rather his justice is not able to rise to its task and, eventually, through zealousness and weakness, it becomes iniquity, petti-. ness, and badness" (p. 101). As will be shown later on, this is a good starting point. Harnack, however, deviates into a wrong direction when he identifies justice and law with the moral law (p. 107/8). He thinks that Marcion does not make the moral good immoral and unjust but, rather, from a religious perspective, degrades moral righteousness to a second-class righteousness; nevertheless, justice and righteousness are supposed to remain an inviolable norm (p. 109). Since, however, the law (i.e., the moral law) does not come from the strange god, Harnack concludes, in pointing to Rom. 7.12: "One is forced to assume that Marcion distinguishes between 'good' and good, 'holy' and holy, 'spiritual' and spiritual" (p. 109). To use scholastic terminology, Harnack understands the relationship as an analogical one, whereas Aland corrected it into an equivocal one in order to preserve the otherness of the strange god.

Harnack works here with Kantian presuppositions insofar as religion does not overturn the moral norms but only transcends them. Yet, how does he support, from the available texts, his distinction between a moral and a religious good? Marcion's antitheses, as far as they are known, do not indicate such a distinction. Harnack relies completely on the reconstruction of Marcion's Bible. He collects all that can supposedly be found in Marcion's Bible that has to do with justice and law (pp. 108-12). I maintain that he draws conclusions from those passages which seem to have been preserved by Marcion. I shall provide evidence for my judgment.

Tertullian is the main witness for Marcion's teaching and work. At the same time, Tertullian is a very able and clever advocate for his own cause, so much so that it is almost impossible to identify in his refutation of Marcion any quotations which are undeniably Marcionite. It is important to know what Tertullian says about his own treatment of Marcion's "purified" test of the Epistle to the Romans: "But how

97

many ditches Marcion has dug, especially in this epistle, by removing all that he would, will become evident
from the text of my Bible. I myself need do no more
than accept, as the result of his carelessness and
blindness, those passages which he did not see he had
equally good reason to excise."[7] We are not furnished
any list of omissions so that the argumentum e silen-
tio cannot be admitted. Reviewing Tertullian's working
method as indicated in the second sentence of the above
quotation, one better relies on his acumen; there is no
use in discovering more contradictions than Tertullian
was able to find. In addition, Tertullian's treatment of
Marcion's gospel shows that he does not only quote from
Marcion's text but sometimes slips into his own. There
are several occasions where he confronts Marcion with
quotations from other than Marcion's gospel texts. An
example is Matthew 5.17. Tertullian says about the second half ("but rather to fulfill them"): "For Marcion
has blotted this out as interpolation" (IV.7.4). Marcion could, of course, well use the corresponding text
in Luke 16.16. It has been suggested that he may have
discussed the passage from Matthew in his Antitheses;[8]
one could also imagine that he included the first half
of the Matthew verse in his gospel. At any rate, extreme
caution is in order for using Tertullian regarding the
reconstruction of Marcion's Bible, comprising also those
passages which Tertullian exploits for pointing out seem-
ing contradictions.

But let us review the proofs for Marcion's understanding of law and justice as presented by Harnack. He
comments on Luke 10.25ff: "Jesus himself here quotes the
law approvingly; Marcion must have held the opinion that
the sum total of the law is correct and right" (p. 111).
The reconstruction of Marcion's text for Luke 10.25ff is
not without its own difficulties (cf. Harnack, p. 206);
however, it is beyond doubt that Jesus refers to the law
even in Marcion's text. I think Tertullian himself provides a sufficient argument for understanding Marcion at
this point; he says: "In the gospel of truth a doctor of
the law approaches Christ with the question, 'What shall
I do to obtain eternal life?' In the heretic's gospel is
written only 'life,' with no mention of 'eternal,' so
that the doctor may have the appearance of asking for

advice about that life, that long life, which is promised by the creator in the law, and the Lord may then seem to have given him an answer in terms of the law, Thou shalt love the Lord thy God...." (IV.25.14), Harnack insinuates: "But Christ put in for those who could understand him the idea 'Ex dei dilectione consequimur vitam aeternam'" (p. 111, n. 1). I find none of that in Tertullian's text.

Much more important is Luke 16.29f, says Harnack (p. 111). Here he relies completely on his reading of the text in which Jesus refers to Moses and the prophets in a positive way. However, even the text reconstructed for Marcion indicates that Marcion's understanding differed markedly from ours. Verses 29 and 30 do not have the subject 'Abraham'; it is also not clear whether Marcion read "in the bosom of Abraham." Be that as it may, Tertullian gives Marcion's interpretation which contradicts Harnack on all counts: "They have there Moses and the prophets, let them hear them." But Marcion twists it into another direction, so as to claim that both of the Creator's rewards in hell, whether of torment or of comfort, are intended for those who have obeyed the law and the prophets, while he defines as 'heavenly' the bosom and the haven of his particular Christ and god" (IV.34.11). This is clear enough, and Tertullian does not furnish any further hint of Marcion's interpretation but rather attempts to refute Marcion on the basis of his canonical text, without taking the elimination of Abraham into account.

Harnack puts special emphasis on the preservation of Rom. 13.9 and Gal. 5.14: "Thou shalt love thy neighbor as thyself." We are probably not less surprised than Tertullian and could well join in his triumphant conclusion: "If this fulfilling of the law comes from the law itself, I am now at a loss as to who may be the God of the law. Perhaps it is Marcion's god" (V.14.13). We have simply to admit that we do not learn from Tertullian how Marcion interpreted Rom. 13.9. I do not think that Marcion wanted to affirm the fulfillment of the creator's law by his unknown god, as Tertullian suggests. It is evident that Marcion attributed direct quotations to the creator and evaluated them accordingly; I believe this can be argued in almost any instance. Tertullian reports on Marcion's interpretation of the same quotation with the same introduction for Gal. 5.14; his introductory formula is typical: "Or else if" (aut si); he uses it after having played his own reading of the text off against Marcion (cf. V.5.6). On Gal. 5.14: "Or else if he wishes 'had been fulfilled' to be taken to mean that it no longer needs to be fulfilled, then it is not his wish that I should love my neighbor as myself--so that this too will have gone into abeyance along with the law" (IV.4. 13).[9] This was Marcion's opinion for which we shall provide further proof. The only puzzle is Rom. 7.12 for which we do not have Marcion's interpretation.

I maintain that the text of Marcion's revised Bible must not be taken by itself for any conclusions; the antitheses are the basis for understanding Marcion's text, although there are some instances where we have to admit our ignorance as to the thinking which lies behind his particular selection of texts.

III. Marcion did not proclaim the love of one's neighbor but the love of one's enemies. His new gospel says: "This is the essential and perfect goodness which is voluntarily and freely poured out to strangers without any obligation of kinship; according to it, we, too, are ordered to love our enemies and, under this designation, strangers" (I.23.3). I have changed Tertullian's indirect speech into direct quotation. There is no word about loving one's neighbor; to the contrary, the love of one's neighbor stands under the obligation from which mankind is promised liberation. I shall explore in this section whether justice and law are surpassed or whether they are negated and superceded by something new. Harnack asserted that justice and law are not rejected in themselves but rather only in the way the creator exercised them. I plan to review Marcion's description of the creator god in order to find out whether justice characterizes him in principle.

Tertullian understood Marcion to say that the law is to be abolished and rejected. In the context of the pericope Luke 18.18-22, he asks Marcion: "Does Christ rescind the former laws that you must not kill nor commit adultery nor steal nor give false testimony

and ought to love father and mother, or does he preserve them and add what is missing?" (IV.36.6) Is the
answer: rescind, or is the alternative wrong? According to Tertullian, Marcion read in the pericope Luke
10.25ff: "What must I do to obtain life? omitting 'eternal', so that the learned man seems to have asked about
the long life promised by the creator and to have responded according to the law, Love the Lord thy God..."
(IV.25.14). Marcion there clearly construes a contrast,
although it is not evident from these passages in what
the contrast to the law consists.

The creator god, according to Marcion, is characterized by qualities which Tertullian summarizes frequently in lists, e.g., pettiness, infirmity, iniquity,
harshness, malice, etc. (cf. Harnack, pp. 269*-272*).
Hatred of Jews has been attributed to Marcion, but it
seems more probable that a definite idea induced him
to the formulation of his antithesis. For why ought the
world to be liberated from the god of the Jews? We
would take Marcion's proclamation on too narrow a basis
if limited to an anti-semitic motif. Rather, the question is, first, what biblical foundation did Marcion
find for his antithesis and, second, how was he able to
find the broad acceptance of the contrasts he mustered?
First, Marcion identified the creator with the lawgiver
whose justice is characterized by jealousy in the first
commandment; such justice is contrasted to the liberal
goodness of the unknown god of the gospel. Second, Marcion recognized, in the actions of the creator god, the
nature of the world to which mankind is subjected in
servitude.

Tertullian does not provide us with any antithesis containing the first commandment as a whole.
Surprisingly enough, however, the concept of jealousy
(aemulatio and derivatives) emerges consistently in
the confrontation with the goodness of the strange god.
"The Marcionites will assert that the essential and
perfect goodness is this: poured out voluntarily and
freely to strangers without any obligation of kinship"
(I.23.3).

Tertullian constructs a threefold argument
(I.23) for refuting the Marcionite proclamation of the
strange god's goodness; he employs a general notion of

God and states that, in God, all that belongs to his essence has to be (a) natural, (b) rational, and (c) perfect. Then he summarizes and demonstrates that goodness is not possible without a judgmental activity--which in turn presupposes jealousy (aemulatio). (a) Natural, i.e., eternal, and here Marcion's god fails because his god reveals himself late in history and did not care for mankind from the beginning. (b) The proof that the goodness of Marcion's god does not meet the criteria of rationability unfolds in several steps beginning with the quotation of Marcion's principle statement about the nature of goodness. The first objection concerns the definition of goodness as love towards strangers. Tertullian argues that, logically speaking, love towards one's neighbors comes first; then, such love can be broadened so as to include enemies and strangers as well. The second objection employs the same argument for the priority of love towards one's neighbor but this time not on a logical basis but rather pointing out the aspect of justice; it is an obligation established by justice to love one's neighbor and kin. Only when this justice has been satisfied can love towards strangers follow "out of the superabundance of justice." By contrast, Tertullian makes very evident what Marcion wanted to say, namely, that love towards one's neighbor is logically prior and that such owed goodness is essential and more dignified. We will not go wrong, I suggest, if we attribute these principles to Marcion's creator god. Yet, Marcion denies categorically the transition from love owed by obligation to love "out of the superabundance of justice"; this is evident precisely because Tertullian wishes to establish a necessary transition from one to the other through the argument of rationability.

The third objection on the basis of rationability relates to goodness realized exclusively towards strangers. Tertullian counters that it could only be rational if it were realized without injustice; but that is hardly the case because the unknown god seizes foreign property and grasps what does not belong to him. This objection attempts to demonstrate explicitly that the savior must be the same as the creator, since love towards strangers implies injustice; the argument works from the aspect of exclusive love towards strangers. The two preceding arguments used the aspect of self-love demanded by justice because it meets a just obligation. Tertullian summarizes both aspects of his demand for rationability of divine justice in the idea of justice: "When, in principle, goodness is shown to its own object, it is rational if just; likewise goodness shown to a stranger is rational if not unjust." If Tertullian is right in contrasting the goodness of the unknown god with justice, then Marcion must have seen justice as such to be irreconcilable with goodness, characterizing the other god, the creator, by contrast.

(c) In addition to the qualities of eternal and rational, perfection has to be attributed to God (I.24). Marcion's god fails in this respect as well; first, not all will participate in salvation and, second, only a part of man, namely, his soul and not his body, will receive salvation. Yet, this is by no means the end of Tertullian's arguments.

Marcion's god does not meet the criteria of the concept of God because of the goodness offered by a new god without obligation. Tertullian wants now to reveal the reason why Marcion refuses to let his god satisfy the general concept of God. This reason is, according to Tertullian, Marcion's definition of God by goodness alone, "to the exclusion of those adjuncts, those feelings and affections, which the Marcionites deny to their god and attach to the creator" (I.25.2). At first, Tertullian speaks of severity and judgmental powers which Marcion denies of his god so that his god becomes similar to the Epicurean deity. Then Tertullian attempts to demonstrate that, precisely of his goodness, a god has to have the wish, the will, and the concern for salvation. At last, Tertullian calls the quality by names which Marcion must admit for his good god and cannot limit to the other god: aemulatio. Neither in logic nor in tradition do I see any reason to put forward against a god of pure goodness just the lack of aemulatio. The enigma is solved if one thinks of the self-presentation of the creator in his law, I am a jealous god who . . .(Ex. 20.5). This must be the quality which Marcion wants to exclude from his god and which he attributes to the creator and his law because it cannot be reconciled with goodness. The activity of the creator as a judge is secondary to and dependent on his aemulatio, it follows from aemulatio. Aemulatio is, according to Tertullian, something like "eager concern, jealous drive of self-realization" (cf. denique volens et concupiscens et curans hominem liberare, hoc ipso iam aemulatur et eum, a quo liberat, adversus eum scilicet sibi liberaturus, et ea, de quibus liberat, in alia liberaturus; I.25.6).

Without jealous concern, God's goodness neither achieves its objective to liberate mankind nor does it acknowledge that, as a matter of fact, it is directed against the creator. God's goodness, says Tertullian, demands that he is "jealously concerned for the good, namely to carry through his will, as well as jealously opposed to evil, namely to eliminate it" (I.26.5).

Tertullian refutes Marcion's description of the creator god in his second book. He is confident of his refutation because he understands God's judgmental activity as his will for education; fear of punishment leads back to the good, and this is the only reason why the creator treats mankind with so much harshness; he wishes to see mankind saved. It this unity of objective between the judging severity and loving goodness of God is once and for all recognized, Tertullian thinks, then Marcion's antithesis can be taken as proof for the unity of the two gods instead of a proof for their disparity. One had only to observe the difference of times: first God is severe with regard to the unrestrained, then he is mild with regard to the subdued (II.29.3). "Thus, it can be better shown by the antithesis that the order of the creator was reformed by Christ than that it was destroyed, regained rather than excluded, whereas you, Marcion, separate your god from every more severe motion, i.e., at any rate from the jealous zeal of the creator" (II.29.3). It is, then, the aemulatio which distinguishes the creator from the strange god of goodness.

IV.   If one wants to find out what makes aemulatio bad, one has to look for its connection with the law. The first commandment says that a jealous god establishes his justice and punishes those who do not obey his law into the third and fourth generation. Justice consists, first, in the ius talionis, as Tertullian elaborates in II.15. Marcion went beyond the law of retribution and exhibited the excessive severity of the creator and lawgiver. Furthermore, his antithesis presented the pettiness, even cruelty and inconsistency of the creator far beyond the mere severity of the law.[10] Does Marcion thereby transgress the contrast between justice and goodness? I do not think so; rather, the law is only the principal instrument with which the creator realizes his jealousy. Tertullian attempts in his refutation to justify God's jealousy; he does this by demonstrating the necessity of God's activity as a judge who actively checks the revolt of mankind against him.

The creator governs through fear; he wants to be feared. In Luke 4.41, Jesus rebukes the demons' crying "Thou art the son of God" and orders them to be silent. Tertullian tries to refute Marcion on his own ground and·presents two arguments. First, Jesus could not have despised the witness of a strange being because neither had he been announced beforehand nor did he have any of his own beings at his disposal to acclaim him; he came as a stranger into the domain of another. Second, Jesus was to be the destroyer of the creator; what could he have wished more than the recognition of the creator's spirits "in fear"? However, as Tertullian continues, Marcion was not able to admit the second point "because he denies that his god is to be feared, asserting that the good god is not to be feared but rather the judge with whom are the instruments of fear, wrath, harshness, judgments, vengeance, condemnation" (IV.8.7). "The judge with whom are the instruments of fear, rage, wrath, harshness, etc." One would expect a contrast between good and bad, similar to the one provided elsewhere: "The bad one will be feared, the good one will be loved" (I.27.3). Yet, Tertullian makes it sufficiently clear that Marcion's principal contrast is not one between evil and good but first and primarily one between just and good, and only secondarily do we find the other predicate: Onerous, burdensome (malus), derived from the just.[11] It does not look as if the judgeship of the creator is attacked but rather the process of judging itself,

105

as Tertullian proves by demanding the quality of _aemu-latio_ necessary for any judge. A judge has at his disposal, as Marcion says, the instruments of fear, wrath, harshness, judgment, condemnation--in no other way can he assert himself as judge; justice is obviously defined by the law which enforces obedience through fear of punishment and hope for reward, as Aristotle, under the impact of Plato, elaborated in a classical manner. The fickleness and inconstancy of the creator is nothing else but the government of a judge who asserts himself (_aemulatur_) by means of the law, fear of punishment, and hope for reward.

Marcion appears to have referred especially to the metaphor of the trees and their respective fruits (_Luke_ 6.43). Origen discusses this Marcionite proof-text in _De principiis_ II.5.4. A bad tree produces bad fruit. The Marcionites to whom Origen obviously refers claimed that the law was the bad fruit and thus revealed a bad god as its author.[12] Tertullian relates the argument of the bad fruit and bad tree with _Is_. 45.7: "It is I who creates bad (evil) things." Although he maintains that Marcion had first found the _Isaiah_ verse and then combined it with the tree metaphor, I suppose that it is possible as well to assume the reverse: the work reveals its author--and too, this god defines himself the same way.

Certainly Marcion did not limit himself to the law but saw the whole world as the work of the creator god. Harnack (p. 273*) is right in commenting: "Yet, ultimately the principal argument for the onerous bad nature of the creator is the world as such." Tertullian provides a quotation from the Marcionites who said: "To be sure, the world is a grand work and worthy of its god" (I.13.2). Marcion pointed especially to the materiality of the world, to the abominable process of creation, even to irksome insects. More than this, the creator god is also attacked with Epicurean argument. Tertullian summarizes (II.5.1-2) Marcion's argument that the creator is a limited god because he is neither good nor fore-knowing nor powerful. John G. Gager[13] has pointed out that this section is identical, even in its details, with a typical Epicurean argument. Although it is possible that Tertullian presses Marcion in his own

106

frame of thought as he does it in the analysis of the goodness of Marcion's good--natural, rational perfect-- the elements of the argumentation show a distinct Marcionite context. "If God were good and knowledgeable of the future and powerful to avert evil, why does he tolerate it that man--his image and likeness, i.e., his substance because of the soul (cf. II.9)--stumbled over obedience to the law into death invented by the devil?" The argument exploits biblical material and is set up to demonstrate the impotence of a creator unable to control his own creature. The law, given later (cf. II.10), does not have any greater power over man; in spite of the law, the elected people often denied their god.

V.   The unknown god reveals himself through the principle of perfect goodness. Goodness is a principle opposed and contrasted to justice in all its aspects. This can only be explained by the lack and absence of aemulatio, self-asserting zeal, through which the creator and lawgiver defines himself in the first commandment. First, goodness is outside of any obligation and is not owed; it is free and voluntary. No kinship may relate its giver with its receiver if goodness is to preserve its essential pure character. The creator is in principle unable to show goodness to mankind; he can only show justice. This is because mankind is his creature and of his substance; to them he owes just treatment and is obliged to provide for them. Self-assertion and self-interest have to be completely excluded so that goodness can come to realization towards strangers alone. For this reason, the good god is by nature unknown (cf. V.16.3). Whatever may be the biblical foundation for such an opinion, Marcion's principal idea can be unfolded on a plain logical basis. Only strangers can be the recipients of god's goodness; otherwise the purity of that goodness will be stained by wrong motives. Marcion could question the creator's command for love of god and one's neighbor because the creator is obliged to care for his creature and man is obliged to love his kin; by justice. The circle of the law is not yet broken by the demand for love and kin' rather, goodness is vitiated by the concern for what one has a right to expect. Self-assertion closes the circle of justice.

Furthermore, it follows from Marcion's principal statement that God reveals himself by himself, and does not reveal himself from the beginning (cf. I.19). The strangeness of the good god is an essential quality because goodness can only be offered to strangers without distortion. One can even say that god was, logically, not allowed to be known before his self-disclosure (cf. V.16.3; also I.11.1), for otherwise his relationship as a stranger would have been lost. Also, the good god cannot reveal himself by means of a creation; for, then, he would put forward something of his own for which he is obliged to show a just concern. Since it is Christ who reveals the new god, the relation of Christ to god is necessarily modalistic.

Mankind is therefore liberated from the enslaving and vitiating obligation of justice and of the law. The work of the good god is the destruction of the creator, including his law. Jesus' actions are interpreted, accordingly, as the breaking of the law; Jesus does what the creator has forbidden (IV.19); the woman with the issue of blood gives witness to her faith by touching Jesus, a gesture prohibited by the law (IV.10). More examples could be given. I think that one has to say that the good god liberates mankind from the world and from the law; he calls men as strangers from out of the world, away from the law. One cannot speak of sin in the traditional sense of the word since it is not an opposition to God; that is, God does not confront mankind with any demand or command (as does the creator god).

The believer, having faith in the good god, is lifted beyond the world and the flesh. Hatred of the world is what alone counts for Marcion's asceticism, as Clement of Alexandria saw so well (Strom. III.3,12.2); libertinism is out of the question because the believer no longer meddles in the affairs of the world. Nowhere does Marcion speak of the law as the means by which evil is averted; the law as such, then, has a limited validity. There is no evidence in his antithesis for not rejecting the law in its moral objective. Believers are transposed into another world where the sphere of morals has become irrelevant since morals have to do with concerns and issues which belong to the world

of the creator. One could, however, take the healings
of Jesus as a surpassing of the creator's sphere,
rather than an elimination of it, because they are
juxtaposed to healings through the history of Israel.
Elisha heals only one leper, but Jesus heals ten;
Elisha employs water, but Jesus heals through his word
(IV.9.8). Yet such antithesis, I think, points more
to the superiority of the good god than to the inclu-
sion of the lesser--the law--into the higher; it does
not exemplify the way in which the law is superceded
by goodness.

Tertullian does not provide us with much information about the soteriological significance of Jesus'
death on the cross. This death is unique to the Christ
of the strange god (III.18); it is curse uttered by the
creator god (cf. III.18.1 and V.3.10 on Gal. 3.13).
The powers of the creator have Jesus crucified because
they want to eliminate a competitor(III.23; also V.6).
Beyond that we are dependent on Ephraim and the references collected by Harnack (p. 288*). From these
one has to conclude that Christ ransoms the strangers
through his death and blood--certainly, one cannot re-
deem what is one's own. In addition, the ransom is paid,
not by a possessive Lord, but in a way which befits the
perfect goodness of the good god, in humility and self-
abasement, so that there can emerge no suspicion of
seizure or usurpation.[14] This is, at least, Marcion's
intention. Here too the motifs of self-assertion and
self-interest (aemulatio) are completely eliminated
so that goodness can reveal itself in its pure form.

VI.   Marcion works exclusively with biblical material; he uses, according to all likelihood, only the
bible of the creator and lawgiver so that one has the
impression that his partners in discussion were only
Christians. The general Christian tradition which Marcion addressed might well be identified with the so-
called early Catholicism which had as its bible the
bible of the Jews. But we know for certain that Christianity was by far more diverse than the later tradition
of "orthodoxy" would suggest. We must also relate Marcion to that complex of traditions which we now call
gnosticism. However, apart from the indication that he

learned to distinguish the "just" god from the "good" god through the teaching of Cerdo,[15] there is little direct support for Marcion's connection with gnosticism. And since we know nothing about Cerdo, even this hint is as much as useless.

It is more rewarding, perhaps, to look to gnosticism itself in an attempt to discover those specific ideas which in this essay have been presented as characteristic of Marcion. At the outset, we find in Irenaeus a report of the teachings of Simon Magus which appear to have a Marcionite flavor: "For man is saved by Simon's grace, not by just works. There are, in fact, no work just (righteous) by nature, rather by accident, inasmuch as the angels who made the world have issued such precepts in order to put man into slavery to them."[17] This statement occurs in a context where the government of angels and demons is to be dissolved by Simon.[18] There are parallels in gnosticism to the bad government of the angels, to their envy and lust for power on the part of the powers of the world, and some of these may very well pre-date Marcion.[19] What is specific in this report about Simon, however, is the indication that the angels usurped and preserved their power by means of the law. F. M. Braun[20] underlines the fact that, in the Irenaean heresiologies, Satornilus says that there were seven creator angels[21] and that the Jewish god was one of them (I.24.1). Basilides gives still another version where he states that the Jewish god is the leader of the creator angels; more than that, the Jewish god intended to subject the nations to his rule with the help of the Jewish people whom he had created (I.24.4). This, too, has a Marcionite coloring. Hippolytus presents the teachings of Basilides in quite a different way; even so, the hybris of the demiurge (Ref. VII.26.3) would not be alien to the report of Irenaeus and can be seen as parallel to Marcion. Braun suggests that both Satornilus and Basilides received inspiration from a common source, namely, the Simonian gnosticism of Menander; further, he believes that Satornilus was directly influenced by Marcionite ideas.[22] By virtue of lack of material and of uncertainty as to precise dates, we are unable to be specific as to who influenced whom. Suffice it to

observe that at least some rudimentary elements of
Marcion's teachings are not foreign to the general
development of gnosticism. I am inclined to give priority to those aspects from Simon, Satornilus, and
Basilides mentioned above, although I do not see any
way of proving it. One could, of course, point out
that the report on Simon in Irenaeus is in indirect
discourse and therefore may be based on some other
source (although not Justin's Syntagma).

The devaluation and even rejection of the material creation is a common gnostic topic, although
there are possible variations such as the conversion
of the demiurge in the systems of Basilides and Valentinus. But as far as I can see, none of these Gnostics
used justice and law exclusively to characterize the
creator god. To be sure, nearly all of them understood
relief from the law as the elimination of the cosmic
law of irrational passions;[23] this, however, is not
Marcion's specific concern. Rather, Marcion understands the law on the basis of aemulatio belonging to
a judge. As such, aemulatio means self-interest.
Therefore, the passions are excluded from the good god,
not because they are a perversion of nature and the
rational order, but because they are instruments of
exercising the law so as to force mankind into the
fear of God. The philosophical discussion of the apa-
theia of God is drawn in[24]--and this should not be
overlooked--but Marcion develops this subject with no
reference whatsoever to the Stoic arguments. In his
far-reaching essay on the background of Marcion's
teachings, J. Woltmann[25] very appropriately mentions
the tradition of discussing the origins of law and
justice, especially among the Sophists and Skeptics.
But he fails to see that Marcion does not simply attribute passions to the creator god and deny that they
belong to the good god, in which case he could employ
Epicurean and skeptic arguments. Rather, Marcion recognizes the judge in the creator, and it is for this
reason alone that the creator god has passions, mate-
ria timoris, because it is aemulatio that makes a
judge.

I think that Marcion, inspired by Paul's rejection of the law as a way towards salvation, has

elaborated the given topic of a lesser demiurge in his own original way. He restricts himself to biblical material and seems to speak only to Christians who keep the creator god as well as the creator god's bible. To this extent, Marcion is a biblicist. But what he says about justice and perfect goodness is his own elaboration. And with the development of this one central idea he addresses implicitly a socio-political theme; his proclamation, therefore, was directed more to the founding of a church than of a school. It is precisely in his biblicism that he speaks on a wave-length understandable to non-Christians. This is because the nature of justice and law is demasked in a general way, not only in the way which the Jewish god exercises them. The Jewish god is, for Marcion, only an illustration of what he wants to critique.

Marcion should not be dismissed by virtue of his having been labelled by Christian tradition as a heretic. Antiquity is replete with instances of doubts about the absoluteness of justice and law; it is a subject of explosive consequences. Compare, for instance, Carnaedes' speech about, or rather against, justice (in Cicero, De rep. III.12-3). Carnaedes said that the mother of justice is neither nature nor will but stupidity; laws are issued in the name of justice but hardly veil the self-interest of the lawgiver. Marcion gives such ideas a new cutting edge in that he characterizes justice and law principally by aemulatio which in turn is contrasted to the goodness the unknown god exercises towards strangers. "The creator lacks merciful kindness and therefore his justice must become severity and cruelty," says Harnack (p. 112). He is wrong. As judge, the creator is by nature aemulus and that is the cause of his severity and harshness.

It is interesting to note that Marcion's disdain of insects has a parallel in the same tradition, e.g., Carnaedes in Porphyry's De abstinentia (III.20 Ip. 210.10ff, ed. Nauck) or in Cicero's Lucullus (38. 102). There one finds an argument against the Stoic claim of a purposeful cosmos: what "purpose" can be found for venemous animals and irksome insects? It seems that Marcion did take up similar ideas and used them to discredit the dignity of the creator god (cf.

112

Tertullian, I.14 and Harnack, p. 270*). But the intensity of Marcion's disgust and abhorrence is new, especially when a heretofore unknown hatred of the world finds vehement expression in his description of the reproductive process (cf. Harnack, p. 273*).

Marcion does not attack philosophers; rather, he wants to persuade mankind that it has to be liberated from the creator god and from his world. The possibility for such a liberation is in the self-revelation of the strange god. "Sufficient to our God is this one single work, that he has liberated man by his great and particular goodness, a goodness of higher value than any number of destructive insects" (Tertullian, I.17.1).

To a world governed and corrupted by self-interest and self-assertion (aemulatio), Marcion's message cannot be irrelevant. He confronts Christian self-understanding with the enormous task of rediscovering an appropriate doctrine of creation. The world as it is experienced does not reveal the good god as its creator but is, rather, devastatingly ambiguous. Any search for a restatement of God as creator will necessarily lead through a discussion of divine justice, what Athanasius, in a later reformulation, refers to as God's truth.[26]

Ekkehard Muehlenberg

113

PLENITUDO HUMANITATIS

THE UNITY OF HUMAN NATURE IN THE
THEOLOGY OF GREGORY OF NYSSA*

The expression "plenitudo humanitatis" occurs
rather frequently in the De divisione naturae of John
Scotus Eriugena. It is a translation of Gregory of Nyssa's phrase (τὸ) πλήρωμα τῆ∫ ἀνθρωπότητο∫. As such, it
symbolizes well the indebtedness of an important medieval idea to a fundamental patristic theme to which the
present paper intends to draw attention. The theme is
the "unity of human nature" or "unity of mankind," and
it possesses profound ramifications and implications
in both theory and practice.

As a historian of this theme in pre-Christian
Greek and Roman thought has remarked:

> In our own day human unity is generally
> seen as a practical problem. We take as
> a self-evident fact the existence of the
> human race as a distinct species, an ag-
> gregate made up of individuals. . . and
> with almost equal readiness most of all
> draw the inference that between all these
> representatives of homo sapiens there is
> some sort of kinship or fellowship which
> should influence their behavior towards
> each other.[1]

But, as some of these practical problems have become
acute, these presuppositions themselves begin to be
questioned--less often explicitly though quite often
implicitly. To reflect, therefore, on one of the
sources of these fundamental axioms of the human community is not only of historical interest but may also be of some contemporary relevance.

Within this short paper I am attempting to make
a twofold contribution to such a reflection of the patristic history of the theme. First, I will examine the

meaning and implications of the teaching of Gregory of
Nyssa on the unity of human nature; second, expanding
the investigation to the sources, parallels and influence of his teaching, I will try to give a more comprehensive panorama of the history and significance of the
theme in patristic and medieval thought. The first part
of the paper is based upon a detailed examination of
all relevant texts of and studies of Gregory--even
though, of course, I can here present only a sketch of
the results. The second part is, of necessity, based
on incomplete evidence and is presented deliberately as
a working hypothesis to be tested by discussion and
confirmed and corrected by further research.

I. The Unity of Human Nature in Gregory of Nyssa

1. The State of the Question[2]

The theme of the unity of human nature in Gregory's thought has been approached by several authors.
Leaving aside the earlier German investigations (many
still valuable, although dated), especially the following should be mentioned: 1) von Balthasar, Rebecchi,
Schoemann, Leys and Ladner have treated of human nature
as created in the image of God; 2) Malevez and Lieske
of the unity of the human nature assumed by Christ;
3) Gomes de Castro and Gonzalez of the unity of the human nature as illustrating the unity of the divine nature (one nature in three persons). Their results are
partial and conflicting. Thus de Castro, for instance,
finds in Gregory a logical unity of nature in the Aris-
totelian sense, Gonzalez speaks of a tendency towards
Platonic realism, while both neglect the texts on the
creation of human nature and its redemption by Christ,
to which in turn the authors mentioned under 1) and 2)
seem to limit themselves, arriving thus at quite different results. Actually, Gregory has much more material on this topic than is usually thought: whereas
Völker (p. 65) speaks of "knappe Andeutungen," there
are, in fact, several hundred passages from all of
Gregory's writings which are explicitly relevant to
the question, and many of these "passages" are in fact
whole chapters or even small treatises. These is also

much more connection between texts taken from the anthropological, christological or trinitarian contexts than the above mentioned authors would realize. Within the limits allowed by such a paper, I would like to sketch, in what follows, these connecting lines.

2. The Themes and their Coherence

a) "Nature" as an indivisible monad

The classical texts for the oneness of human nature are found in the so-called "minor dogmatic works" of Gregory--Ad Graecos: ex communibus notionibus and Ad Ablabium: quod non sint tres dii--in which he rejects the alleged tritheistic implications of the divinity of the Son and of the Holy Spirit. Among other arguments--notably that taken from the perfect unity of the three Divine Persons in their operation--Gregory affirms that not even in man, or for that matter in any other species, is the "nature" as such multiplied.

> Our first point is this: To use in the plural the word for the nature of those who do not differ in nature, and to speak of 'many men,' is a customary misuse of language. It is like saying there are many human natures. That this is so is clear from the following instance. When we address someone, we do not call him by the name of his nature. Since he would have that name in common with others, confusion would result; and everyone within hearing would think that he was being addressed. For the summons was not by an individual name, but by the name of a common nature. Rather do we distinguish him from the multitude by using his proper name, that name, I mean, which signifies a particular subject. There are many who have shared in the same nature--disciples, apostles, martyrs, for instance--but the 'man' in them all is one. Hence,

as we have said, the term 'man' does not refer to the particularity of each, but to their common nature. For Luke is a man, as is Stephen. But that does not mean that if anyone is a man he is therefore Luke or Stephen. Rather does the distinction of persons arise from the individual differences we observe in each. When we see them together, we can count them. Yet the nature is one, united in itself, a unit completely indivisible, which is neither increased by addition nor diminished by subtraction, being and remaining essentially one, inseparable even when appearing in plurality, continuous and entire, and not divided by the individuals who share in it.

Just as we speak of a people, a mob, an army, and an assembly always in the singular, and yet each of them entials plurality, so even the term 'man' should properly and most accurately be used in the singular, even if those we observe to share in the same nature constitute a plurality.[3]

This affirmation may be striking, but it is by no means isolated in Gregory's works. As a matter of fact, in most cases when he argues against the subordination of the Son to the Father by the Arians (esp. in his Contra Eunomium) or of the Spirit to both Father and Son (esp. in Contra Macedonianos), the same doctrine is affirmed, although not in such complete a form. But whereas in the "minor dogmatic works" the accent lies on the oneness of nature in the multitude (πλῆθος) of individuals, in most other texts Gregory underlines the fact that the common nature (φύσις) or essence (οὐσία) is found in each to the same degree, for nature (essence) does not admit of "more or less."[4]

In these texts, too, the difference between the divine unity and the unity of created species is further illustrated. For even though created intellectual (intelligible) beings (i.e., angels and human souls) do not differ in sensible quality as do created material things, nor do they differ as to their nature (essence) from each other, they do differ as far as they partake more or less of the goodness of God. The Son and the Holy Spirit, however, are good, not by participation (that would imply composition, peccability, etc.), but by essence and differ only in their mode of procession from the Father.[5]

b) The "fullness" (πλήρωμα) of mankind

There is, however, in Gregory's writings another approach to human unity which, emerging in a different context, does not seem to harmonize with the preceding conception. The classical text for this view is found in the De hominis opificio, commenting on Gen. 1.27 ("God created man, in the image of God he created him, male and female he created them.") Gregory's difficulty is the manifold discrepancy between man's historic condition and the perfection expressed by "image of God" (for "in Christ Jesus there is neither male nor female"). His solution to the problem, presented as a hypothesis, is as follows:

> In saying that 'God created man' the text indicates by the indefinite (τῷ ἀορίστῳ) character of the term all mankind (ἅπαν τὸ ἀνθρώπινον). For Adam was not here named together with the creation as in the story that follows, but the name given to the man created is not the particular (ὁ τὶϚ) but the general (ὁ καθόλου). Thus we are led by the employment of the general name of our nature to some such view as this: that in the Divine foreknowledge (προγνώσει) and power all humanity (πᾶσα ἡ ἀνθρωπότηϚ) is included in the first creation. For it is fitting of God not to regard any of the things made by Him as indeterminate, but that each existing thing should have some limit and measure prescribed by the wisdom of the Maker. Now just as any particular man is limited to his bodily dimensions, . . so I think that the entire plenitude of human-

ity (ὅλον τὸ τῆς ἀνθρωπότητος πλήρωμα) was
included by the God of all, by His power
of foreknowledge, as it were in one body,
and that this is what the text teaches us
which says, 'God created man, in the image
of God he created him.' For the image is
not in part of our nature, nor is the grace
in any one of those things found in our nature, but this power extends equally to all
the race (ἅπαν τὸ γένος). A sign of this is
that the mind (νοῦς) is implanted alike in
all: . . . the man that was manifested at
the first creation of the world, and he that
shall be after the consummation of all, are
alike: they equally bear in themselves the
divine image. For this reason the whole race
(τὸ πᾶν) was spoken of as one man, namely
that to God's power nothing is either past
or future, but even that which we expect is
comprehended, equally with what is at present existing, by the all-sustaining energy.
The whole nature (πᾶσα ἡ φύσις, then, ex-
tending from the first to the last, is, so
to say, one image of Him Who is (μία τις
τοῦ ὄντος ἐστιν εἰκών); but the distinction
of kind in male and female was added to His
work . . .[6]

Here it would be wrong to argue, as several authors
have, that this is an isolated text. True, Gregory never repeats this whole explanation of this text in its
details, but he not only did not repudiate it in later
works; he actually presupposes it in several of his
arguments.

(1) Double creation. Does Gregory's text teach a
"double creation" and thus two different "original
states" of mankind, an angelic and an earthly? Gregory's
constant teaching on the nature and vocation of man as
an intermediary uniting the intelligible with the sensible seems to exclude a purely angelic state. Corsini[7]
has convincingly shown, on the basis of a clear paralel-
lism between the texts of the De hom. op. and In Hex.,

that instead of "two creations" we should speak of "one creation only, instantaneous, global, and above time on the part of God, which develops within the dimensions of space-time (διάστημα) on the part of the creatures."[8] Correspondingly, there was, historically, only one original state (even though, as we shall see, in speaking of the "resotration of the original state, Gregory has primarily God's original--and final--plan in mind).

(2) The meaning of the term πλήρωμα.[9] Since this term has been so widely used in the literature on Gregory, it is surprising to find that its precise meaning has not yet been analysed. Actually, Gregory uses the term in several meanings, most of which are of doctrinal importance.[10] The examination of the term in the above passage and in parallels shows, I think, that here πλήρωμα means the "whole sum," i.e., the "complete number" of individuals; in the case of the πλήρωμα τῆς ἀνθρωπότητος, the complete number of men (foreseen by God).[11]

(3) Parallel expressions. The same meaning is expressed by Gregory by a whole range of parallel expressions found in De hom. op., such as πᾶσα ἡ ἀνθρωπότης (16.44, 185B), ἅπαν τὸ ἀνθρώπινον (16.44, 185B), ἅπαν τὸ γένος (16.44, 185C), πᾶσα ἡ (scil. ἀνθρωπίνη) φύσις (16.44, 185D; 17.44, 189C; 22.44, 204D), ἡ καθόλου φύσις (22.44, 204D), τὸ τῆς φύσεως πλήρωμα (22.44, 204D), πλήρωμα τῶν ἀνθρώπων (22.44, 205D), ἅπαν . . . τὸ ἀνθρώπινον πλήρωμα (29.44, 233D). These expressions are by no means confined to De hom. op., but are found throughout Gregory's works.

Furthermore, in an essentially analogous sense, Gregory speaks also of the πλήρωμα of other beings (wherever a determined full number is referred to).[12] Of special interest for us are those texts which speak of the πλήρωμα of angels or even of the whole rational nature[13] (which seems to include both angels and men).

c) The coherence of the two conceptions of the "unity of human nature"

In most of the studies on the themes examined above, it was taken for granted, without further thorough examination, that the conceptions of human unity described under a) and b) are simply identical or simply different. Without going into all the ramifications of the problem, it can be shown, I think, that the two conceptions do indeed differ, but do not contradict each other.

They differ as to the meaning in which some of the terms, especially φύσις , are used and, correspondingly, as to the dimension (or aspect) of reality which is emphasized. For φύσις(used as a synonym for οὐσία) in the minor dogmatic works, as well as in (many) parallel texts, is used, to put it simply, with primary attention to the "intension" (content, connotation) of the concept, and in this sense the specific nature (e.g., ἀνθρωπότης) does not admit of degree or division. The same term φύσις, however, as used in De hom. op. 16 and parallels--usually, but not always, modified by πᾶσα--is used with primary attention to its "extension" (denotation), i.e., as referring to the whole class of individuals who share in it, and in this sense consists of the "parts" (individuals or groups of them). It is to be noted that, as far as I can see, οὐσία is used as a synonym for φύσις in sense a), but never in sense b).

The teachings, however, underlying conceptions a) and b) are not in contradiction, but in harmony. For in the texts under a) also, the unity of nature did not exclude but rather included the multitude (πλῆθος) of individuals (ἄτομον, ὑπόστασις) partaking of it even though it did not refer to them directly. In sense b), φύσις is used to refer indirectly to the multitude of individuals, but individuals which (or who) are united by partaking of the φύσις in sense a). The term πλήρωμα (or the adjective πᾶν, πᾶσα) indicates that it is the "numerically complete" or "whole" multitude which is referred to, not any particular group.

Viewed in this light, the two sets of texts illuminate rather than contradict each other. They also

122

clearly converge in another important respect: in excluding the conception of a nature or οὐσία which would be conceived as above (outside of) the individuals sharing in it. The φύσις (οὐσία) in sense a) is one in many--but there is no indication that it would be conceived by Gregory as having a reality of its own apart from them. The πλήρωμα of mankind or the whole "nature" in sense b), which may seem to be at first sight distinct from the individuals, is indeed their sum (therefore Gregory has to refer repeatedly to the foresight of God in order to explain how, from the point of view of God, the whole nature can be created at once).

3. The Themes in their Applications and Implications

The applications and implications of this theme (or of these two corresponding themes) in Gregory's writings are so manifold and extensive that their systematic analysis would entail an exposition of his whole theology. Let me simply indicate, therefore, the main lines and call attention primarily to some neglected or misunderstood points.

a) God and creatures: 'Theologia'.[14] The (very extensive) use of the theme of one nature (or essence) in Trinitarian theology, for all its real or alleged ambiguities, has helped Gregory to profess the sharing (κοινωνία) in one nature without subordination. At the same time, combined with his doctrine of "vertical" participation of intellectual creatures in God's perfections, Gregory's conception of human nature (and, generally, of created intellectual nature) enabled him to maintain an unwavering distinction between God and His creatures: there is a communion of nature within the Trinity and within mankind, but between divine nature and human nature, or rather created rational nature in general (which includes human souls) there is an essential distinction, and there is, further, no "intermediary" (μέσον).[15] Jesus Christ, however, is a true Mediator (μεσίτης), precisely by his being truly and fully both God and man.

b) <u>Salvation history: 'Oikonomia'</u>. The solidarity of mankind, as expressed in the two conceptions analyzed above, is an underlying presupposition of the whole drama of salvation (as conceived by Gregory), beginning with creation and ending with the consummation of all (ἀποκατάστασι𝑓). Given the richness of the material, only selected points can be given here.

(1) <u>The Fall of 'Man'</u>. It is a widely accepted view that "original sin" in us (peccatum originale originatum) is alien to the Eastern Fathers. Such a generalization, however, is based largely on the explicit or tacit presupposition that only the views of·Augustine, as developed in the Pelagian controversies, merit that name. There is, also in pre-Augustinian Eastern patristic thought, nevertheless a clear consensus as to an "original" fall of man which deprived him of his special communion with God and in which somehow all men participate. Such a view pervades Gregory's works, too, and is constantly based on the same fundamental premise: in the first man (or men), who was the only representative of mankind, the whole of human nature has somehow been separated from God. Let me quote here (in part) one of his most complete texts (taken from <u>De or. Dom.</u> 5), commenting on "Forgive us our debts" and dealing with the problem of those who would not be conscious of personal sins:

> Let not him who is inclined to such an opinion speak impertinently like that Pharisee who did not even know his own nature. For had he known that he was a human being, he would have learned from Holy Scripture that his nature was by no means pure from defilement, for it says that there cannot be found among men one who lives without stain one day. . . The passage enjoins us not to look at the things which have been accomplished but to call to mind the common debt of human nature in which everyone included has a share, because he participates in the common lot of man's nature, and to beseech the Judge

to grant forgiveness of sins. . .
For since Adam is, as it were, living in us,
we see each and all these garments of skin
round our nature, and also the transitory
fig leaves of this material life which we
have badly sewn together for ourselves after being stripped of our own resplendent
garments. . . Having been wrapped up in
these things, let us imitate the Prodigal
Son after he had endured the long afflic-
tion of feeding the swine. When, like him,
we return to ourselves and remember the
heavenly Father, we may rightly use the
words: Forgive us our debts. . .
Hence, even though one be a Moses or a
Samuel, or any other man of outstanding
virtue, in so far as he is a man, he does
not consider these words less fitting for
himself, seeing that he shares Adam's nature and participates in his exile. For
since, as the Apostle says, in Adam we all
die, the words that are suited to Adam's
penance are rightly applied to all who have
died with him, so that after we have been
granted the remission of our sins we may
again be saved by the Lord through grace,
as says the Apostle.[16]

(2) Incarnation and Redemption. "Gregory has
worked out more precisely than Athanasius . . . the application of Incarnation--but naturally with the help
of a completely Platonic thought. . . Christ did not
assume an individual human nature, but the human nature.
Correspondingly, in Him the whole human nature grew together with the Divinity; the whole human nature became
divine through the inmixture of the Divine."[17] These
words of Harnack are central for his understanding of
the soteriology and theological anthropology of the
Greek Fathers. The view expressed by them is still influential, even though Harnack himself was forced to
admit that, according to Gregory, Christ did assume an
individual human nature which included somehow the
whole human nature, and that Gregory was "not only a

Platonist but also a Biblical Christian."[18]

In fact, there can be no doubt that Gregory conceived the Incarnation to be the Son of God becoming an individual man (without ceasing to be God). In virtue of the unity of human nature, however (and Harnack is partly right here), in and through Jesus Christ the whole of human nature is restored to communion with God. The underlying idea is far from being "completely Platonic," for--as we have seen--even the conception of nature as an undivided monad in many is not simply Platonic; furthermore, Gregory uses, in the majority of texts, the conception of nature as the fullness of all individuals (see above 2, b)). Nor did Gregory conceive of redemption as accomplished simply by the Incarnation, for, as he says in a central text from the Or. cat.:

> . . . the death did not occur because of
> the birth, but that, on the contrary, the
> birth was accepted by Him for the sake of
> the death. He who eternally exists did not
> submit to being born in a body because he
> was in need of ·life. Rather was it to re-
> call us from death to life. Our whole na-
> ture had to be brought back from death. In
> consequence he stooped down to our dead
> body and stretched out a hand, as it were,
> to one who was prostrate. He approached so
> near death as to come into contact with
> it, and by means of his own body to grant
> our nature the principle of resurrection,
> by raising our total humanity along with
> him by his power. . .
> Not from another source, but from the lump
> of our humanity, came the manhood which
> received the Divine. By the resurrection
> it was exalted along with the Godhead. In
> the case of our own bodies the activity
> of one of our sense is felt throughout
> the whole system which is united to it.
> In just the same way, seeing that our na-
> ture constitutes, as it were, a single liv-
> ing organism, the resurrection of one
> part of it extends to the whole. If, then,

He who stands upright stoops to raise one
who has fallen, what is there in our religious teaching which is outside the realm
of probability?[19]

Nor does Gregory see our restoration "as a
strictly physical process."[20] For, first, the "death"
from which we were liberated is certainly not our "sensible reality" (Sinnlichkeit)[21] but alienation from God,
as the "life" in which salvation consists neigher simply nor primarily in the incorruption of the body but
in personal communion with God.[22] Secondly, although
Christ's death and resurrection have re-united all humanity virtually[23] with God, this communion has to be
actualized by faith in, and sacramental and moral
"imitation" of, Christ.[24]

(3) Final restoration: 'Apokatastasis'. Gregory's understanding of the unity of human nature, and
even of the whole created intellectual (rational) nature, also underlies his teaching on the final return
of all to God. First, the very notions of "restoration"
or "return" need qualification. For the "original state"
which is "restored" at the end is not that of the first
individuals (Adam and Eve) in paradise, but that of the
fullness of humanity as conceived in God's eternity, of
which the historic existence of Adam and Even was but an
inchoate anticipation (soon lost by sin).[25] Thus Gregory's notion of salvation history is that of a temporal
realization of an eternal (in the strict supra-temporal
sense of the word) divine design, and, instead of a
cycle, its symbol would rather be an ascending line,
or perhaps a spiral.[26]

Second, in spite of much hesitation on the part
of ancient and modern authors,[27] one has to admit that
several of Gregory's texts--notably those ex professo
treating of the final consummation--affirm the final
restoration of all rational creatures to God (including
not only all men but even the fallen angels). Certainly, Gregory sees this return, not as an automatic fact,
but as a long educative and purificative process. There
are elements in Gregory's thought which have been worked out by Maximus Confessor in a synthesis in which the

final consummation is maintained along with the assertion that some rational creatures are definitely alienated from God.[28] It is, however, not clear to me that Gregory has anticipated this view in anything more than a very groping fashion.

II. Sources, Influences, and Further Implications

If the applications of a major theme in Gregory's theology to specific elements within it have been treated in a very selective and summary fashion, this will be even more true in this final section where I hope to present his views in a more comprehensive panorama. For Gregory's speculations, original as they may be at several points, reflect a common patristic tradition and were, in turn, influential upon subsequent Eastern and Western theology.

1. Sources

The main source for the doctrine of the unity of mankind is, first of all, the universalism expressed in the Old Testament's teaching on creation, human history, and the Messianic hope, a universalism which was later consciously emphasized in the New Testament (especially by Paul). Another very important factor in the development of the doctrine was the struggle against heterodox Gnosticism. It was in this context that Irenaeus[29] stressed against the Gnostic division of men into separate classes (whose fate was essentially determined by their original make-up), the unity of mankind. He affirmed this, both in the sense that each man is created (in respect to his body and rational free soul) in the image of God, each called to that perfection which consists in becoming like God and thus truly alive by participation of the Spirit, and in the sense that God's plan of salvation in Christ, the second Adam, includes the whole human community. It was a strong anti-Gnostic concern, too, that motivated Origen to insist on the fundamental equality of all rational creatures, all of whom are "unius naturae secum invicem uniusque substantiae,"[30] differ only in consequence of the various uses and abuses of the God-given freedom. There indeed can be no doubt that these views of Irenaeus and Origen were known to and influential upon Gregory.

Philosophical ideas too have played their part-- secondary, but important. The Stoic doctrine of the basic equality of all men partaking of the same logos was wide-spread and easily assimilated and transposed by Christians, as was also the Stoic idea of a cosmic solidarity.[31] As a matter of fact, both Athanasius' and Basil's views on the "consubstantiality" among creatures and men (as an analog for the consubstantiality in the Godhead) seem to be of a more Stoic that Platonic mold.[31]

Thus "Platonism" was certainly not the (only or main) source of the patristic doctrine of the unity of human nature. This does not mean, however, that the Platonic tradition, especially Middle and Neo-Platonism, did not have a great influence on its linguistic and conceptual formulation. Gregory of Nyssa's teaching, in particular, of the one undivided nature in a multitude of individuals seems to be indebted to the New-Platonic commentaries on Aristotle's logical works, notably Porphyry's Isagoge, in both terminology (see, for instance, the word πλῆθος for the individual instance) and context.

It has nevertheless to be noted that the philosophical terms and ideas of Platonism were not simply taken over; they were transformed and inserted into a synthesis that was of a fundamentally Christian inspiration. It is for this reason that we can say that Gregory's distinction of two types of participation is something relatively new, even from the philosophical point of view.

2. Influences

That the patristic doctrine of the unity of human nature has been influential upon subsequent Byzantine and Western medieval thought is obvious. I would like to draw attention to only one aspect of this influence, one which has thus far--in my judgment--received insufficient attention. The medieval problem of "universals" has too often been seen to have philosophical origins; I would argue that these origins are primarily theological. Marius Victorinus and Boethius were, respectively, not only translators of and commentators on Neo-platonic logical works, but also authors of important contributions to the theology of the Trinity. They and their readers were preoccupied with the human solidarity underlying salvation history and symbolizing the unity of Divine Persons. Anselm of Canterbury, asks, for instance, "how can someone who does not yet understand how several men are one man in species comprehend how in that most mysterious and lofty nature several persons, each one of whom is perfect God, are one God?"[34] In particular, the position known as "immanent realism," i.e., that universals are real but do not exist apart from individual instances, can be traced back to patristic theological origins.

As to the specific influence of Gregory of Nyssa, there is one channel through which is has been unquestionably present: John Scotus Eriugena.[35] He translated, as had Dionysius Exiguus before him, Gregory's De hominis opificio into Latin under the title De Imagine, and his own theological anthropology, developed in the De divisione naturae, is full of quotations from and reflections of Gregory, including Gregory's concept of the unity of human nature in its various forms.

3. Further Implications

Finally, I can touch briefly on the implications which the patristic doctrine of the unity of human nature have had for the social and political realm.

a) The implications are rather obvious for a theology of the church. Indeed, if most Eastern Fathers did not develop a distinct "ecclesiology" per se, they nevertheless developed very much the communitarian dimension of the whole "economy" of salvation. In this perspective, the "Body of Christ" is the "whole of mankind," even though the transformation brought about by Christ has not yet been actualized in all.[36] It would be worth investigating further to what extent this outlook has been reflected in practical Church attitudes (in missionary activity, as one of but many examples).

b) Another implication of the doctrine of the unity of human nature lies in the realm of social morality. If human nature is the same in all, although deprived of higher divine gifts but not corrupted in its essential content, and if human nature has, furthermore, been restored (virtually) by Christ, then we have a foundation for moral law which is valid for all and which presupposes an equality of human dignity. It is thus that we find in the works of the Fathers the beginnings of a Christian theory of "natural law" and of "natural rights,"[37] as well as concrete applications of this theory for practical conduct (as illustrated, for instance, by Gregory of Nyssa's homilies "de pauperibus amandis").

c) Lastly, I can only ask the question as to whether and how far the doctrine of the unity of human nature has had implications for political theory, notably in respect to the ideal unity of the empire, and to theories of the relationship of Church to State.[38]

It is impossible, however, within the scope of this paper, to do more than raise the questions which are implicit in the material we have looked at. As an historian of ideas, however, I have tried to understand a vitally important doctrine as it is developed both by an early Christian thinker and by the scope of early Christian tradition. To evaluate this doctrine in detail, both philosophically and theologically, would be a fascinating task. What I have written thus far is but a prologomenon to that task. It is, however, perhaps not out of place to remind ourselves that--although we may at times be in a position to judge, correct, and improve upon the views of past ages--this does not dispense us from answering for ourselves the question of the nature, meaning and purpose of human solidarity. It is my conviction that it is precisely in respect to this question that we can still learn a great deal from the early Christian understanding of man, all men and women, as created in the image of God.

David L. Balas, O. Cist.

PROLEGOMENON TO A STRUCTURAL ANALYSIS

OF ANCIENT CHRISTIAN VIEWS OF SALVATION

The idea of salvation has held, practically from the outset, a major place in the Christian church. The concept sōteria, the model sōtēr, and the verb sōzō are found abundantly from the letters of Paul to the last documents of the Patristic age. Similarly, the concept "soteriology," the model of a "redeemer myth," and the designation of Christianity as an Erlösungsreligion have for a long time been basic models for research into ancient Christianity. And yet there is hardly any agreement as to what "salvation" actually is, or was, either in antiquity (where different concepts of salvation stood side by side, from Mark, Luke, and John to Arius, Athanasius, Augustine, and Cassian) or in modern scholarship (from Cardinal Newman to Harnack and Seeberg). While the concept of a redeemer myth has remained a useful research tool for some, this very term is scoffed at by others; and while the primal issue between Arius and Athanasius, for instance, has often been seen as one between ontology (Arius) and soteriology (Athanasius), the same controversy is evaluated differently by Groh and Gregg.[1] It was an accurate description of the evidence and of the scholarship when Donald Winslow, at the International Patristic Conference in Oxford (1975) coined the term: "soteriological jungle."[2]

I propose that the discrepancies, contradictions and confusions in the salvation language of the ancient church belong to one basic "salvation schema," a structure of language, thought and action which makes no sense in terms of a consistent theory of salvation, but which can be successfully analysed in terms of binary components. Even though the statements about salvation appear confused, they reveal a consistent subsurface structure, and are part of a symbolic system which becomes comprehensible when we relate its polarizations to each other.

1. In order to discover a structural system, such as salvation might reveal, it will be wise not only to look for the content of a sentence in which "salvation" appears, but for the relation between the sentences in which "salvation" appears. The content of two salvation-sentences might differ, but there might be a relation between the sentences which can be specified.

2. We might discover a common underlying dynamic even in two statements which are quite contradictory to each other on the surface level.

3. A person might speak about salvation when he speaks about something else. The issue and the problems of salvation might be present in sentences and statements which do not contain the word-group sōteria.

4. A person might combine two different salvation statements because he wants to communicate something that is not contained in either one of them.

5. The word sōteria could function on several levels, ideological as well as political. To talk about salvation might mean a different thing for the bishop than for the layman who hears the bishop.

6. If we are faced with conflicting statements and related models, we must look for specific social, historical, and existential causes. When a Christian makes two heterogonous statements about salvation, he may do so because he has had two different experiences.

7. Language is action, not merely reflection. We must try to find out to what degree a man reflects and to what degree he acts as he employs the language of salvation.

8. In a major religious movement, it does not suffice merely to examine social, ideological, legal, and ethical models. A symbolic system not only operates with models of language but also with models of vision, with iconic units.

The following four sections of this paper will attempt to provide an outline of the problems involved in an understanding of sōteria.

In searching for a salvation schema in the texts of the primitive Christian church, we detect three basic patterns which are employed time and again, not only by different writers but also by one and the same writer. The first pattern contains the primal alternative, implied in the original use of the word, between "salvation" and its counterpart, non-salvation; or, as Phil. 1.28 formulates it, "perdition"; the alternatives are between healing and non-healing, health and sickness, remaining sick and getting healed, joy and damnation, blessing and cursing:

$$\boxed{p} \,\text{-------------------}\, \boxed{s}$$

some are lost   some are saved

In Lk. 6.9. (cf. 19.10): is it allowed, on a sabbath,

to destroy a person   or to save him?

In 1 Cor. 1.18:

the word about the   it is the power of
cross is foolishness   God for us who are
to those who are lost   saved.

The polarization is found in another form in the exclamation of the disciples during the storm (Mt. 8.25):

we are lost (drowning)   save us

It is also found in Pauline variations, such as Rom. 8.11 vs. Rom. 8.2:

sin has seduced and   the law of the spir-
killed me   it has made me free

One might include the alternative between "old" and "new," for instance, in Mk. 2.22:

old wine is destroyed   new wine/new skins

Or the many kingdom passages, such as <u>Mt</u>. 10.6-7:

> go to the <u>lost</u> sheep of   preach: the kingdom of
> the house <u>of Israel</u>   heaven is at hand.

The alternatives include different people:

> he invited many (who   (instead he said) go
> did not come; <u>Lk</u>. 14.16   into the highways and
>   invite them; <u>Lk</u>. 14.23.

They distinguish between many and few:

> many are called; <u>Lk</u>.   few are saved; <u>Lk</u>.
> 13.24   13.23

In the distinctions between many and few, several variations can be seen, in the parable of the sheep (<u>Lk</u>. 15.4),
for instance:

> <u>ninety-nine</u> sheep   <u>one</u> sheep

or in the eschatological parable of <u>Mt</u>. 25.1-23:

> <u>foolish</u> virgins   <u>wise</u> virgins

or even the reverse, <u>Mt</u>. 25.14ff:

> <u>one</u> useless servant   <u>two</u> good servants with
> with one pound   five and ten pounds

The alternatives proclaim judgment, as in <u>Jn</u>. 3.16:

> he who <u>does not believe</u>   he who <u>does</u> believe
> is already judged   will not be <u>judged</u>

final separation between human fate, as in the story
of the two criminals at the cross; <u>Lk</u>. 23.39ff:

> one criminal at the   the other defends Je-
> cross blasphemes Jesus   sus and is saved

exclusivity, as in <u>Acts</u> 4.12 <u>vs</u>. 4.10:

in no other name is	the paralytic has been
there salvation	healed in the name of
	Jesus

a poetic vision of death and its reversal, as in Mt. 28. 3-4:

the guardians at the	the angel was like
tomb became like the	lightning and his
dead	cloth like snow

a precarious hope, as in Mk. 13.20:

nobody would be	unless God shortened
saved	the days

and a final apocalyptic alternative, in Rev. 21.8 and 21.3:

the second death	the dwelling of God
	with man.

These examples are a first set of evidence for Winslow's "soteriological jungle." The texts speak about healing and preaching, saving and judging; they express value judgments, social separations; they point to the past and to the future; they consist of words, events, and theological concepts. But one common denominator is found in these examples. Salvation implies a distinction, a separation, between people, between values, between issues, between times. The primary separation is between two kinds of people:

some people are lost, sick, drowning; they die, they are seduced, they live in sin, they are judged, they end with blasphemy on their lips;

some people are saved, they are healed, they do not drown, they will be in paradise (even today); they will be cleansed, they live, they are made new, they will live in the kingdom.

137

To sophisticated soteriological minds, trained by centuries of theological discrimination, such a distinction sounds trite and simplistic. Indeed, simplistic it is. There exists in ancient Christianity an alternative between salvation and damnation (perdition), an alternative that appears in many forms, one that can be traced through all the NT texts from the Synoptic Gospels to the Book of Revelation.

A second pattern that can be isolated in primitive Christian texts distinguishes between an acting, or active, component (saving) and a passive component (saved). It consists of two forms:

$$s^{act} \qquad\qquad s^{pass}$$

someone saves   someone is saved

or, in the neutral form:

something saves   something is saved

The first consists of personal, the second of impersonal models. The two can be mixed: somebody saves something; something saves somebody. On the left side, I list the following in abbreviated form:

$$s^{act}$$

God saves the Son (Jn. 12.27)
God saves those who believe (1 Cor. 1.21)
God saved us (2 Tim. 1.5)
God saved Christ (Heb. 5.7)

Christ came to save sinners (1 Tim. 1.15)
Jesus saves his people (Mt. 1.21)
The Son of Man came to save (Lk. 19.10)

if I (Paul) may save some (Rom. 11.14)
that I may save some (1 Cor. 9.22)
you will save yourself and those who hear (1 Tim. 4.16)

the prayer of faith will save the sick (Jn. 5.15)

138

On the right side, the following examples may be given:

_spass

Jesus says to God: Father
save me (Jn. 12.27)
Christ the High Priest is
saved (Heb. 5.7)

Paul is saved (1 Cor. 1.18)

The Christians are saved (1
Cor. 15.2)
the believer (Acts 16.31)
the gentiles (1 Thes. 2.16)
the demoniac (Lk. 8.36)
the people (Mt. 1.21)
a human being (Mk. 3.4)

the spirit (1 Cor. 5.5)
no flesh (Mt. 24.22)
the cosmos (Jn. 12.47)

I have listed sentences only where the word group salvation appears. These texts do not contain any kind of
classical soteriology. Both of the components contain
personal as well as abstract models--God, Christ, and
Paul on one side, spirit and cosmos on the other side.
The mediator appears on both sides, but so does Paul!
The examples do not give any answers to later soteriological problems, such as the relation between God and
Christ, or salvation by Christ or by works. But the
texts have one common denominator: something happens
(or has happened, or will happen) to someone. It happened to Christ and to Paul. It shall happen to Christians. Just as in the first pattern the content of salvation was not clear, so in the second pattern the
agent of salvation is not clear. What is clear is the
relation between saving and saved. A change is implied.
An event. A deed. The modern observer may claim, from
his own dogmatic presuppositions, that in all of them
God is the agent of salvation. By implication this may
be so. But the texts do not say so. The texts clearly

139

name God in some of the examples and not in others; they name prayer and faith in some of them, and that puts an entirely different face on soteriology. The structure is ambiguous, and the ambiguity is well expressed in the text of 2 Tim. 2.4: he wants to save all . . . so that I may save some. It is not more ambiguous than the material presented in the two tables above.

A third primitive Christian pattern can be isolated in which a distinction is made between people, deeds, models from which one is saved, and people, deeds, models to which one is saved:

$_s$from	$_s$to
we are saved from	we are saved to

Acts 2.40-1:

| let yourself be saved from this generation of darkness | into the community in which three thousand were baptized that day |

2 Tim. 4.18:

| The Lord will save me from every evil work | and preserve me unto the heavenly kingdom |

To this duality belong all the healing stories of the Synoptic Gospels and of John. A person is saved:

| from sickness, paraly-sis, demons | to health |

and the change is expressed by the phrase: "your faith has saved you" (Mk. 5.34, 10.52; Mt. 9.22; Lk. 7.50, 18.42). The pattern can deal with concrete physical events, as in the story of Peter walking across the water when Peter was, in fact (Mt. 14.31-3) saved

| from the water | into the boat |

but it can also contain theological models, as in Rom. 5.9-10:

<u>from</u> wrath	<u>to</u> a state of redemp-tion

The pattern appears in many transformations which employ metaphors of running, changing, hoping. A good example is <u>Phil</u>. 3.13-21 which has, for instance, the following three transformations:

leave things behind	reach for things before us (3.13)
change our vile body	that it may be fashioned like unto his glorious body (3.21)
there are enemies whose end is destruction	I press toward the mark for the prize (3.14)

As with the first two patterns, this pattern, too, emerges from the heart of the primitive Christian experience. Jesus came to heal people, to bring them from sickness unto health. He brought the disciples from Galilee to Jerusalem and was to lead them back to Galilee (<u>Mk</u>. 14.28). Paul's life's work was to lead people from their present (Jewish or gentile) life toward the day of Jesus Christ (<u>Phil</u>. 1.6). The terminology fluctuates. We have to deal with images as well as with words. Not only verbs like "to save," but also "to heal," "to gain" (1 <u>Cor</u>. 9.20-2). The components belong to various kinds of models. There is a physical change: Jesus saves the five-thousand from hunger. There is social change: The Jews are saved as they become Christians. There is existential change: toward hope (<u>Acts</u> 27.2) and eternal life (<u>Mt</u>. 19.17). But all components belong to one underlying dynamic: Christians (in our case, Christian texts) communicate to others that a person can (or did, or should) change <u>from</u> negatively described people, forces, actions, states of being, <u>to</u> positively described people, forces, actions, or states of being.

This trifold structural salvation schema represents the framework within which the ancient church, and the Christians within that church, could function and grow, and through which one could find what was promised--a new sense of life. For newness is indeed the first common dynamic behind these three patterns. Two forces work against each other, perdition and salvation. The most ancient Christian texts do not make it unequivocally clear from what the Christian was being saved, or had been saved; himself, sickness, the world, the Pharisees and Sadducees, the prince of this world, sin, error. Nor is it unequivocally clear to what he has been, or is being saved; God, Christ, faith, community, health, eternal life. Yet, as we take the three structural patterns together, a picture emerges. Given the alternative between salvation and its opposite, a person had a chance. Somebody had come, was coming. People could go, went, were going from one to the other. There was "old" and there was "new" and there was movement from one to the other; there were agents that helped in this movement; and there was a receiving community.

The dynamic of the schema was change. Social change: from the Jewish world at large to the Jewish-Christian sect, from the diaspora community to the Christian community, from the gentile culture to the Christian sect. Ideological change: from traditional beliefs and values to Christian beliefs, creeds and stories and liturgical formulae, from darkness to light, from scripture wrongly understood to a new understanding of scripture. Existential change: from fear of death to expectation of resurrection and eternal life. Mythic change: from the reality in Satan and the prince of this world and darkness to the Kingdom of God, the church, Jesus Christ, the Spirit.

The dynamic expressed the move toward a uniqueness, of belief as well as of movement. What happened here did not happen elsewhere, in no other name. But here it did happen, concretely, today (Lk. 19.5), once for all (Heb. 6.4). It was no innocent play: the savior over life and death was judge. Some will not make it (Mt. 24.20).

The schema can be documented from the oral traditions behind the Synoptics, and hence worked for people in general as well as for sophisticated individuals such as Paul and the author of the Epistle to the He-

142

brews. It could be used by the pictorial community of, say, Mark, as well as by the expository languages in Romans. We do not ask at this moment if the pattern was believed totally, if the carriers of these sentences meant to communicate other things than those we have stated. As the sentences stand, they were the backbone to any ancient Erlösungs-religion. They gave man a way to look at his past (we were lost), at his fellow believer (we are saved), and at the rest of the world (believe and you might be saved!).

Within such a salvation schema, the term SOTERIA soon became an abstraction, a word-symbol that could be used without outside, complimentary components. The Christian did not have to spell out in what his salvation lay or who the agent of the salvation was. It was simply salvation. Salus. The term is vacillating and ambiguous. It leaves open the subjects and objects, the means and goals of salvation. It implies that people knew what the term pointed to. Perhaps they did; perhaps they did not. Soteria implied a great many things, as even the earliest texts indicate: a new recognition (Lk. 1.77), a new kind of life for Greeks and Jews (Rom. 1.16), a new uniqueness (Acts 4.12), a new way (Acts 16.17). Later on in this paper we shall see that the fluidity and vacillation of the concept of soteria was indeed almost indispensable. The cryptic abstraction, soteria, was useful, nevertheless, to the earliest Christians who were able to say, if need be, who their savior was, and knew the community to which they were saved. They also knew many of the words of Jesus and words about Jesus which expressed their faith in salvation.

II

As we turn to the succeeding centuries, during which Christianity grew into a world religion, we can trace the threefold salvation schema in numerous texts. Just a few examples must suffice to indicate the trend.

As to the first pattern (p-s), from the first Christian manual, the Didache, to the medieval judgment in Torcello, Christians continued to operate with a

143

juxtaposition of perdition and salvation, phrased in a variety of ways:

p: s:

The Didache and the Apostolic Constitutions propose two ways:

the way of death the way of life

From Revelation to Cyprian, there is

Anti-Christ Christ

Polycarp, the martyr of Smyrna (Mart. Pol. 2.3; 9.3) juxtaposes:

everlasting punishment by a single hour the
reserved for the un- martyr purchases eter-
godly nal life

Lactantius, not in the martyr tradition, proposes the same alternative (Inst. IV.11):

penalty of death reward of life

The apologist Aristides (Apol. 17) offers Christians:

escape from punishment and they shall be
and condemnation found heirs of eternal life

The popular texts are as important as the intellectual documents. They contain extremely vivid descriptions of the salvation-perdition pattern; so, for instance, the Latin version of the Gospel of Nicodemus (9.25):

the descending savior and others he led
throws people into Tar- with him to the up-
tarus per world

A similar setting forth of the salvation-perdition theme is found in the Acts of Philipp:

144

an abyss opened and	the place where the
proconsuls and priests	apostles stood with
were sunk into it	their kind remained
	unshaken

A vision in the Acts of Thomas renders the alternative with the imagination of a modern horror film:

there was a chasm with	and the people laid
women who were devoured	their sick on the
by worms; there was ano-	road; when Thomas
ther chasm where people	came by, he healed
were hung up by their	them.
tongues.	

These texts are somewhat later than the ones given above, but they document the extraordinary popular sadism expressed in imagining the alternatives facing mankind. In its ultimate judgmental quality, if not in its crudity, the popular vision is paralleled by the sophisticated North African, Tertullian, whose Exhortation to Chastity (13) leads either:

to concupiscence,	or to paradise
and there is no	
paradise in that	

Another transformation of the schema was the autobiographical construct in which the past becomes a tortured, terrible time where man is lost, as opposed to the present, where he is saved (Clem. Rec. I.3ff; Clem. Hom. I.3ff; and, of course, Augustine, Confessions).

The alternative has many transformations and meanings. I only mention, among others, the harshness of the martyr's choice (Act. Just. 5):

the most terrible judg-	"our salvation"
ment seat of our Lord	

(and "our salvation" means, of course, the "victory" of the martyrs, their death and reward); the poetic beauty in Ignatius' alternative is characteristic (Eph. 19-20)

145

| magic was abolished | we shall not die but live in J. Chr. for- ever |

There is an ethical alternative in Athansius (De inc. 3):

| if they transgress they must suffer death | if they remain good they have life in paradise |

It is important here to mention an event which had pro- found influence on the future of Christianity. At the beginning of the fourth century, with Constantine's victory over his foes, a new triumphant age dawned (Lactantius, De mort. pers. 1):

| foes are destroyed; the enemies lie low; torturers die under torture | the clouds of the past are dispelled; God the Almighty has manifested his power |

The exuberance ceased to exist rather soon, but the idea that indeed with the Constantinian age something new had arrived changed the pattern for the rest of the patristic period. Perdition and Salvation had been po- litically resolved with Constantine, and that convic- tion (no matter how illusory) came as a second compo- nent along side the belief that, with the coming of Jesus, the victory had been won. We shall return to this problem later.

As for the second pattern (s^{act}-s^{pass}), the am- biguities to which we pointed before continued through- out the patristic age. They produced the major ideolo- gical conflict, the christological and trinitarian con- troversies of the 4th and 5th centuries. The controver- sy was clearly an attempt to resolve in which way $\underline{s^{act}}$ was God and Christ. The controversy arose also because the Christians never successfully combined their salva- tion schema with their creation schema. We do not have to dwell on this conflict except to point out one im- portant thing. Fourth century Christians tried to re- solve the ambiguity, the vacillating structural, mythic, intuitive pluralism of the original Christian s^{act} component. The result was not a solution but a transformation of the component into somewhat more philosophical models: one essence, three persons. But responsible for that transformation were two factors which have to be separated from each other. On the one hand, the people who transformed the early Christian symbols and enforced Nicene and post-Nicene models were the very intellectuals who demanded a resolution of the contradictory and unsatisfactory pre-Nicene content structure. On the other hand, the people who responded to the change, intellectuals or non-intellectuals, were people who demanded an absolute primacy of divinity in the s^{act} component of the salvation pattern. In a sense, the basic structural relation remained the same, even for Arius. Salvation was still a deed by someone (even though it was hard to say simply and unequivocally who the agent was), done to someone else. And that someone else was still the Christian, in the church, believing in the salvatory schema, living it, acting it out. Some bishops got deposed; others committed crimes because of the disagreements. The salvation structure per se was not changed in the age of Constantine. Only centuries later did the early Christian schema, under powerful influences from without as well as from within, begin to collapse. But that development belongs to a period long after the one under present investigation.

In the evolution of this second pattern, another set of transformations can be traced. Even in NT texts, the active agents of salvation were not limited to God and Christ; Paul, too, saw himself as a salvific agent. He tried to save, convert, or, as he puts it (1 Cor. 9.20), "gain" or "win" people to salvation. For Paul, then, there was a personal involvement at work in his transmission of salvation, and thus an element of power and authority: even if an angel were to proclaim another gospel . . . (Gal. 1.8)! The human authority, already at work in the primitive time, is constantly sharpened, augmented, and clarified during the subsequent two centuries. "Where the bishop is, there is the Catholic Church" (Ign., Smyrn. 8.2). The traditional interpreter of patristic material is quick

147

to protest against any "soteriological" meaning behind such words. He is surely wrong. He has been trained to separate theological categories from concrete political or social ones, ignoring the fact that a soteriological statement is a concrete one, born of a situation, and the situation, for Ignatius or anyone esle, is rooted in and is a part of the dynamic of power and conflict. "If someone is in Christ, he is a new creature" (2 Cor. 5.17); this Pauline phrase is rooted in the social reality of Paul and of the communities of which he was a part. Paul had joined a new community. It brought him agony, beatings, hatred, jail. The Ignatian sentence goes farther only in degree, not in kind. Instead of the "apostle," the "bishop"; instead of an emerging primitive congregation, the "Catholic Church" (whatever Ignatius may have meant by those words). Ignatius demanded obedience of the bishop in the same way that Paul demanded obedience. For both, it was ultimately obedience to Christ; yet for both, obedience to Christ meant obedience to their own person, in the church: "even if an angel from heaven were to proclaim another gospel . . ."

The familiar words of Cyprian make the character of the transformation clear. "You cannot have God as your father, if you do not have the Church as your mother" (De un. 5). If this is not a statement on the salvation of the Christian, what is? After all, in the same treatise, the church is the ark, and the people in the ark are (ever since the beginning of the church) the people who are saved. The image of the boat (ark) goes back to the story of the boat on the Sea of Galilee (and ultimately, of course, to the story of Noah). What happens in this development is that the s^{act} components receive more authoritarian weight, more hierarchic power. The bishop has become the élite representative of the Christians. The transformation from early Christian to middle patristic tests indicates clearly the rise of episcopal power, the growth of numbers, and the increase of influence; but the same structural schema is at work.

The salvation pattern can lead to militancy. Cyprian speaks about Christ looking down on his soldiers as they fight. He uses the Pauline metaphor of the "helmet of salvation." And ahead of the soldier lies the "joy of eternal salvation" (Ep. 58.8). This transformation into a political, and even military, metaphor of aggression was surely a serious change from the primitive salvation schema of the apostolic age. Here it is that we see the transformation that lies behind the subsequent appeal to the Christian religion of salvation for the ideological support of war and murder in the name of religion. It is a shock to realize that a similar primitive schema of salvation lies behind both religious attitudes. A structure of change can serve more than one purpose; to preserve the structure itself is no guarantee of moral consistency.

Nevertheless, the transformations we have been speaking of also serve the very opposite of militancy. Antony sells his belongings. Virginity is praised as the highest good. From Pachomius to Augustine, Christians live a life of discipline, they create special communities, and they praise celibacy. Asceticism could, to be sure, be employed in the service of episcopal hierarchy, as Athanasius demonstraes. Canon 18 of the Synod of Elvira shows a very close realtion between asceticism and episcopal power.[3] Yet there are groups of Christians leaving for the Egyptian desert who do not play the game of clerical power, but who enact the salvation pattern in their own, anchorite, individualistic, world-denying fashion.

Behind the s^{act} component of this pattern we can trace a threefold structural ambiguity:

(a) the ambiguity between: "God saves the world" and "Christ saves the world";

(b) the ambiguity between: "God (or Christ) saves man" and "man is a savior to his fellow man";

(c) the ambiguity between: "you are saved by someone" (i.e., God, Christ, Paul, the bishop, the church) and "you are saved by what you do" (i.e., belief, prayer, ascetic life, poverty, virginity).

149

Behind s<u>pass</u> is hidden, as I shall show in
Part III, the most explosive and structurally most discordant polarization in the schema of ancient views
of salvation. As for the third pattern, s<u>from</u> – s<u>to</u>,
the polarity of change and differentiation, a few examples will suffice:

> that he might revive   by their appropria-
> men from death   tion of his body and
>   by the grace of the
>   resurrection (<u>Ath.</u>,
>   <u>De inc</u>. 8)

Ignatius, <u>Tral</u>. 7:

> from impure   to pure

<u>Clem</u>. <u>Rec</u>. II.71:

> unclean   clean

<u>Clem</u>. <u>Rec</u>. II.18 (as a metaphor for the step from
ignorance to reason):

> you enter a smokefilled and open the door and
> room   let the sunlight in

<u>A</u>pos. <u>Const</u>. VI.30:

> from Jewish washings   to reading books,
>   singing for the dead
>   martyrs, offering the
>   Eucharist

and also (V.15):

> from the madness of   to true monarchy
> polytheism

In popular acts, the alternative in the arena was (<u>Act</u>.
<u>Thecl. et Pauli</u>.):

> to be saved from nakedness to being clothed

Methodius has both a mythic alternative (<u>Symp</u>. 8.12)

　　　　dragon　　　　　　　　　virgin

and, like the <u>Gospel of Thomas</u>, a sexual change (8.8):

　　　　from female　　　　　　　to male.

At this point I wish to identify four ways in which ancient Christians understood or used such a salvation pattern:

(a) They constantly created a <u>social</u> polarization (e.g., the Jews had only a dumb lamb; we have the blood of the New Covenant: Ath., <u>Fest. Letter</u> 4.3). There were imaginary foes in the past, such as the Pharisees ard Sadducees, or Simon Magus. There were foes in the present, such as the Valentinians, Judaizers, the Catholics (for the Donatists), and the Donatists (for the Catholics).

(b) There is a constant <u>creedal-ideological</u> polarization. Many of the texts were written because someone (e.g., Ignatius, Irenaeus, Athanasius) meant to talk people into accepting the right faith and prevent them from being deceived by erroneous ideas. The Nicene church wants to force people to move from heresy to orthodoxy. Constantine would help to enforce this desire.

(c) There is an <u>existential</u> polarization. People desparately want to go from death to life, from fear of corruptibility to an assurance of resurrection, to eternal life and immortality.

(d) There is also a constant polarization of <u>life-style</u> and <u>social order</u>. The Christian went from Jewish washing to Christian washing; from the Sabbath to the Day of the Lord; from fasting Mondays and Thursdays to fasting Wednesdays and Fridays; from circumcision to baptism. He no longer went to the Temple and the arena, he went to church and basilica. The bishop of Rome attempted to force churches in Asia Minor to move from their Easter cycle to the Roman cycle.

Material such as this, of course, could fill many volumes. I wish simply to point out some of the significant aspects. There exists a double vacillation between the ambiguities of the pattern. First of all, vacillation goes on within one and the same issue. For example, Paul of Tarsus had at least three separate existential hopes: he wanted to be·with Christ, he wanted to remain alive for the sake of the church, and he looked for the resurrection of the dead at the parousia (Phil. 1.23-4; 1 Cor. 15.20ff). More than this, he spoke of a mystical experience, of being caught up into the third heaven (2 Cor. 12.2ff). And as he went on to explain what physical resurrection was, he had to resort to metaphors such as the death of the seed before it could bring forth life, indeed another expectation as to life after death. The lively debate as to whether it is physical or spiritual resurrection, immortality or recreation of the body, misses the point. Immortality and resurrection were equivalent to being "with Christ," and each were interchangeable components over against death, lostness, and alienation.

A second vacillation goes on between different polarizations. Athanasius, for example, was fighting a social battle for his metropolitan see of Alexandria, against Jews and Arians, against all kinds of other Egyptian foes, against rival metropolitan and episcopal competitors. The salvation schema is surely part of that battle. But Athanasius was also fighting for a concept of salvation which had its own inner consistency (whether or not the modern interpreter would agree as to the degree of consistency!): if Christianity is a religion of salvation, then the Savior himself must be fully divine. This was the battle which

152

which Athanasius fought on the spiritual front, and it is beside the point how successful he was in this. And elements appropriate to this struggle were his admiration for Antony, his high regard for virginity, and the discipline with which he conducted his own life in the midst of turbulent affairs.

The examples just referred to come from two highly intelligent leaders of the ancient church, albeit three centuries apart. The texts are addressed to other Christians, to rival Christians, or to specific individuals. And it is important to take into consideration that the overwhelming majority of our texts were written by members of the Christian élite (i.e., apostolic, episcopal, intellectual, or ascetic élite) and not by the laity. The texts transmit an insight or story or a recollection. Someone should hear, should change, should be attacked, or should be comforted. However, when we have, as in the Apocrypha, some access to the "average" Christian, we discover a much more simplistic, at times even grotesque, vision of the dynamic of salvation. But the primary texts, on the whole, reveal the concerns of the élite. It is no coincidence, therefore, that the extant early Christian texts which speak of salvation represent the emergence of clerical power, and this power is expressed in terms of control and submission:

admonish the people that they are saved (Ign., Pol. 1.2)

be submissive to the bishop and to each other as Jesus Christ was to the Father, and the Apostles were to Jesus Christ (Ign., Magn. 13)

These two statements are made, on the one hand, to a fellow-bishop and, on the other, to the laity of Magnesia. They both contain a hierarchical trend: control and submission, authority and order. Salvation is inseparable from obeying someone, from controlling someone. And it is significant that Ignatius has Jesus Christ, the mediator, in both roles. There was no agreement in the early church as to the exact nature

153

of authority--was it apostolic or presbyterial, episcopal or conciliar, metropolitan or patriarchal? Paul,
the elders, Justin Martyr, Pachomius, Leo of Rome,
Origen, Cyril of Alexandria--all had differing ideas
of authority. But the trend is unmistakable. The more
the church received power, the more the need arose to
spell out the specific forms of control (the Synod of
Elvira and the Nicene controversy are ready examples).
It is no coincidence, then, that the age in which the
control of the élite over the church reached its apex
was the same age in which the battle over the correct
meaning of salvation broke out.

It would be a mistake not to underline one
crucial aspect of this relationship between patterns
of salvation and the patterns of control, namely, the
element of fear. We have already pointed to the alternative between paradise and hell, punishment and reward, eternal joy and everlasting torture. The struggle between the orthodox and the heretic is the struggle between Jacob and Esau; as Cyprian knowingly asserted, "you may lose your birth-right" (Ep. 73.25).
The unjust and intemperate, said Justin Martyr, shall
be punished by eternal fire (Apol. II.1). And the
bishops of Elvira (Can.1, etc.) demanded that a person guilty of a serious crime should not receive communion, even if on his death-bed. The salvation schema
worked, in effect, because people were afraid and
therefore susceptible of control.

III

Only now can we turn to the fourth structural
problematic of ancient Christian salvation language.
It is the most serious one, qualifying and modifying
the previous patterns. What I have presented thus far
represents the base for any ancient religion of salva-
tion--Christianity, Isis, Mithra, Cybele, etc. Man is
taken from this world into a symbolic new world of
myth, liturgy, and community. Priests, mystagogues,
or leaders take him, through initiation, into special
sacred places where he receives new life, feasts at a
banquet, and experiences rebirth. But it is the fourth

154

pattern of salvation which distinguishes Christianity from these other religions. The specific nature of Christian salvation lay not only in the church's political and cultural drive, in its aggression, exclusivity, and intolerance, but in a pattern which created from the first decade onwards a considerable amount of agony; it is the pattern which consists of two statements about man's salvation:

$_s$past $_s$future

we have been saved   we shall be saved

This duality is found in the Synoptics:

the girl arose and   no sign shall be given
walked around; she was   to this generation
twelve years old (Mk.   (Mk. 8.12)
5.42)

today, salvation has   today you shall be
come to this house   with me in paradise
(Lk. 19.9)   (Lk. 23.43)

today, the savior was   He is not here; he
born (Lk. 2.11)   is risen (Lk. 24.6)

they recognized him   and he disappeared
(Lk. 24.31)   (ibid.)

And in the Gospel of John (15.11 and 16.12):

I have told you that   I would have much to
my joy may be perfect   tell you but you
in you   could not tolerate
                            it now

And in Paul:

we have been justified we shall be saved
and have peace with   (Rom. 5.10)
God (Rom. 5.1)

155

we have died with Christ	we shall live with him (Rom. 6.8)
we were buried with Christ	so we might walk around in newness of life (Rom. 6.4)
the law of the spirit has made me free (Rom. 8.2)	God will make your mortal bodies alive (Rom. 8.11)

The first sentence says something happened--to me, to us, to you, to them. What happened consists of many forms--physical or symbolic events, the arrival of Christ, health, salvation. The second sentence says something shall happen. It does not say then--today, soon, in the future, when Jesus will return, when the Paraclete will be sent, when the end and last judgment shall come.

On the one hand: Your faith has saved you (Mt. 9.22).

On the other hand: The one who will endure to the end shall be saved (Mt. 10.22).

We find, in fact, two salvations. One is a past event: people were changed (2 Cor. 5.17); a star shone and magic was dissolved (Ign., Eph. 19). The other event lies in the future: resurrection, parousia, judgment, to be with Christ. It will come like a thief in the night (Mt. 24.36), at the last trumpet (1 Cor. 15.52); nobody knows the hour.

One can explain this duality by creating some kind of soteriological system. Christ has saved us, but fulfillment lies in the future. Such an explanation may have answered the needs of later Christians but it does not do justice to the polarization expressed in the texts. One could also point to the Stoic doctrine of moderation, or the mixture between virtue and vice; to the paideia of the Greeks (as found, for instance in Irenaeus, Origen, and others). But neither educational progress nor a doctrine of

156

moderation sufficiently explains the extraordinary polarization between these two salvation assertions. No one of these assertions claims (as could a later gloss) that "Christ has done it already and will conclude his work at the end." Nor are these assertions statements about intellectual or moral growth.

We get closer to an understanding of the problem by taking seriously the textual expressions themselves, and by placing them into their concrete historical context. The Christian movement began with certain events and words. A man from Nazareth lived, spoke, assembled disciples. Something happened. People heard and saw. Paul had seen (1 Cor. 9.1); the author of the Gospel of John spoke about seeing (3.11); the woman who came down from Galilee saw (Lk. 23.49). The person they saw, spoke to, or heard about, spoke about the future, about the kingdom of God, about resurrection and return. So people who were around him and followed him spoke also about the future. Scholars will never fully agree as to what is authentic either in the life of Jesus or in the words attributed to him about the future. But one thing is beyond doubt: no matter the exact historical sequence, and no matter how accurately certain words were attributed to Jesus, the church began as a movement of people who looked back to the Jesus who expected the kingdom to come. This structural polarity is therefore the result of, and absolutely intertwined with, the primal experience of the movement's beginning:

we have seen	we shall see
mine eyes have seen your salvation (Lk. 2.30)	they shall see God (Mt. 5.8)
She had seen the Lord (Jn. 20.18)	we shall see him as he is (1 Jn. 3.2)
have I not seen the Lord Jesus (1 Cor. 9.1)	there (in Galilee) you shall see him (Mt. 28.7)

157

Yet even these sentences are not merely statements about actual past events or anticipated future events. The past had already become symbolic. Lk. 2.29, for instance, is an early Christian hymn; Jn. 20.29 is an interpretation of the resurrection "event"; 1 Cor. 9.11 is a statement by a person who had not known Jesus. This hermeneutic process began at once: words and deeds that went back to the time of Jesus were recalled, understood, augmented, reshaped, and translated by people of a subsequent generation. The words and expectations about the kingdom became part of the same creative process. Memory and creativity went together; a pattern was created which juxtaposed a salvation that had happened in the past with a salvation that was yet to come.

In order to understand this pattern, we have to isolate its two components. Each of them was spoken with a seldom expressed but often implied polarity. On the left side, the statement about the salvation which had come to Christians and to the world was, even in the age of Paul, qualified by an awareness that it had not really happened. In an uncomfortable way, something of the perdition, of the non-salvation component, was still operative in the present:

$_s$past	$_p$present
you are (were) saved	but you did not act it
you were washed, sanctified, justified	but some of you are thieves, drunkards, etc. (1 Cor. 6.9-11)
the Lord took bread	whoever eats it in an unworthy manner will be guilty (1 Cor. 11.23ff)
you were sincere and innocent	but now . . . (1 Clem. 2.5)

158

| no one should possess anything | but since many of you have possessions (Clem. Hom. 15.9) |

The ancient church continued this pattern throughout its entire history. The age of the apostles was better than the present age; then there were signs and miracles, but today they no longer occur. The church created its canon out of this division between the better primitive Christian past and the less good Christian present.

But there is a second polarization which we can also trace back to the very earliest texts. The present is indeed difficult, but the future will be different. There will be justice, final mercy, and salvation. While the present is problematic (i.e., a mixture of salvation and perdition), the future will be pure salvation:

$s + p$ present	$_s$ future
things are not as they should be	there will come a final salvation

For instance,

the church in Corinth has within it a dreadful sinner who should not be tolerated;	he should be surrendered to Satan so that his spirit can be saved (1 Cor. 13.12)
now we see through a glass darkly	but then face to face (1 Cor. 13.12)

or the eschatological parables:

| wheat and chaff | harvest (Mt. 13.24ff) |

or the writings to the churches in Asia Minor:

| the church in Laodicaea is to be spewed out of my mouth | the one who conquers will sit with me on my throne (Rev. 3.16 and 21) |

159

This entire eschatological dynamic, evident from M̲t̲.
24 to D̲i̲d̲a̲c̲h̲e̲ 16 and throughout similar passages of
later times, belongs to this distinction. Too, the
emerging ethical and penitential developments similarly
belong to the same division:

although the gates of mercy are have been closed	God allowed some opening, namely one single additional penance (Herm., M̲a̲n̲d̲. II. 2.5)
there are certain sins of daily life to which we are all liable, and if there were no pardon for them, there would be no salvation--	and there will be pardon for them through the intercession of Christ with the Father (Tert., D̲e̲ p̲u̲d̲. 19)

The alternative was developed not only within the penitential framework but in general ethical models as
well:

when you are sunk in the waves of sin	clutching to the plank will raise you up (Tert., D̲e̲ p̲o̲e̲n̲. 4)

In both of these sub-patterns, the past-future polarization is broken up by the present--a difficult present, mixed and at times outright bad. The fourth
structural pattern of the salvation schema, then,
looks like this:

$$\underline{_s\text{past}} \quad \text{-------} \quad _s\underline{\text{future}}$$

$$\underline{_s\text{past} \; \text{-} \; _{sp}\text{present}} \qquad \underline{_{s+p}\text{present} \; \text{-} \; _s\text{future}}$$

Even in this picture, counter-dynamic elements have to
be considered, such as the statements (R̲o̲m̲. 7-8; C̲l̲e̲m̲.
R̲e̲c̲. 13) that the past was worse and the present is
better, or (M̲t̲.24) the prophecies that the future
will, at first, once more be terrible.

160

But why should this structural complexity indicate a qualification? Simply because it interrupts the liturgical and mythic sequence of a full-fledged salvation religion: Christ is risen; if someone is in Christ, that person is a new creature; the old has passed away. Paul founded one new community after another, only to see them torn apart by inner strife (1 Cor. 1.12). He had to learn the hard way that healing was not to be a completed process, for what he saw in these primitive communities was sometimes ugly (1 Cor. 5 and 11). And half a century later the author of the Apocalypse (Rev. 1-3) saw good things as well as bad, so he was certainly realistic in assigning any real change or any real solution to the future. It was clear that the full change which was celebrated in the mythic and ritualistic language of salvation had not in fact taken place. People were certainly given a new identity and a new sense of life, a new community and a new ideal; but newness was intricately mixed with conflict, with ugly discord, and with rivalry even between major apostles. The mythic sequence, in a word, was not true; or, at best, it was only partially true.

As we watch the centuries of growth from the time of the apostles to the age of Nicaea, we discover that the starting-point for the whole mythic system-- the first alternative between perdition and salvation-- returns into the midst of the salvation people. Christians threw rather ugly anathemata against other Christians, against Valentinus, Marcion, Arius, Apollinaris, and Nestorius. The canons of Elvira, eighty-one of them, not only severely disciplined some of the believers but mercilessly threw many of them out. North Africa (and soon thereafter, Egypt) was in turmoil because vast groups of Christians slandered other groups, even to the point of violence and murder. What started as a mythic construct of "newness" ended in the same agonizing mythic and social conflicts with which the movement had begun, except that the conflict between inside and outside had, by the time of Nicaea, become the conflict among Christian believers. This latter state differed from the earlier only in degree: in its militancy and in its political means and scope. The conflict arose precisely from the salvation schema

161

in which were found the kernels of turmoil:

$_p$perdition _ _ _ _ _ _ _ $_s$salvation

$_s$act _ _ _ _ _ $_s$pass

$_s$from _ _ _ _ $_s$to

$_s$past _ _ _ $_s$future

$_s$perdition_ $_s$salvation

This qualification and modification of the salvation
sequence was not the result of a seminar in patristic
and New Testament soteriology. It was the result of
sometimes half-conscious, sometimes repressed feelings. It has a great deal to do with the problem of
illusion versus social and ethical honesty, a problem
that poses itself for any religion or movement of
salvation. The church of Nicaea, for example, claimed
that it only "vindicates irreproachable characters"
(can.9). That sentence is simply not true. Look at
Eusebius of Caesarea; look at Athanasius; each of them
on opposite sides of the christological conflict.
Nobody was to point this out, at least not during the
council proceedings. Nobody would relate the incred-
ble statement of canon 9 to soteriology. Linguistic
processes evolve in a much more subtle way. Because
such statements were felt--must have been felt--to be
only partially true, salvation statements were qualified. Hence, the future; hence, the optative; hence,
the doctrines and practices of penance, from Hermas
to Cassian.

Because salvation statements were qualified
and not taken in a pure and uncompromising way, the
early idea of salvation led to and was a part of a
considerable amount of anxiety. A religion of salvation promises rebirth, initiation, new life, banquet
and joy. Instead, the history of the first four
Christian centuries reveals a picture of hatred and
schism and anathemata alongside the glory, joy and
beauty. The qualification of salvation language both
points to and reflects great tension. Is it not

ironic that the "saved" should be so tense? Nietzche's famous dictum comes to mind: "they should look more saved, should we believe in their salvation." Our paper has shown that anxiety is indeed a part of the salvation structure; the schema would not be so confused, so "torn up," were this not so. Behind the glorious dynamic of Paul lay an uncertainty that lies behind all his writings, from Romans 7 (even if he were to speak only about his past, my schema has shown that the past is involved in the present!) to his very position as an apostle (2 Cor. 10ff) and to his final admission that he has not reached his goal, but that he was still running after the prize (Phil. 2). Behind the dynamic of Augustine, four centuries later, lay a similar anxiety about his past, about the efficacy of grace, about the Donatists whom he meant to extinguish, and about the Pelagians whom he hoped to defeat.

Christianity brought with it a schema which represented, along with its Jewish past, a broken system, for all the intellectual and existential astuteness of its founders. The patristic development is not a "fall" away from New Testament times but only a sharpening of conflict. With the rise of episcopal power and with the growth in numbers, anxiety increased; with victory over the pagans, the conflict became internalized--the victim was now to be found inside the churches not outside. But basically this qualification was present during Christianity's first generation; otherwise Paul would not have written that he came not to baptize but to preach the Gospel (1 Cor. 1.17). The qualification of salvation belonged to the very schema itself of Christian salvation.

That the Christian would qualify his very own salvation was expressed in one of the crucial models which the ancient church perpetuated, namely, the double reversal of the life and death metaphor:

he who loses his life -- shall gain it
and he who wants to
gain his life   --   shall lose it

The first set is perfectly comprehensible, given the sequence of death and rebirth; but the second set

qualifies the Christian's search for precisely that
life which is promised in the first set. This double
sentence expresses the kind of qualification which
we have found in the whole schema. The Epistle to Diogne-
tus formulates the qualification in another way:

the Christians have a common table	and yet not common
they obey the estab-lished laws	and in their own lives surpass the law
every foreign land is to them a fatherland	and every fatherland a foreign land

The qualification and ambiguity of salvation acted as
the ever-present counter-agent in the Christian religion's rise to power. One cannot build a hierarchy on
the conviction that one who wants to gain his life
will lose it. The Christian salvation schema contained
and tolerated such a qualification. This duality may
have made people anxious; it certainly made the churches vital!

IV

The ancient Christian salvation schema has a
center: the model of the Savior. Without considering
the Savior as a mythic model or as an icon, any analysis of soteriological language would not only be incomplete but also outright misleading. The Savior
does more than illustrate social and ideological presuppositions (as a one-sided intellectualist observer
might assume); he carries the system. Early Christianity has, at its center, the person of Christ. This
person combines the elements we have outlined in the
previous three sections. He was born and he died. He
rose, in the past, and shall return, in the future.
He became man (an act of Incarnation) and suffered
(an act of Redemption). He suffered and he won; he
cried out and he conquered; he was God . . . and he
was Man.

The myth of the Savior combined those elements which the ancient church, and the individual in that church, experienced in tension. The tensions present in the Savior model helped foster one schism after another. The Church never fully agreed on the description of its Savior. It did not have to. He appeared to be one--he had a name, even though the code-names used to refer to him were in constant transformation from the earliest to the latest times: Son of Man, Rabbi, Son of God, Word, God, Pantocrator. But iconically, at a given moment, the God-Man figure was not a conglomorate of words--he was one in name and in shape. The Christians had, of course, a whole string of saving models attached to the Savior--intellectual, political, disciplinary, sacramental, mystical. But never did they say: "We have a number of saviors who effect different salvation and speak to different salvation problems." No, they had one Savior.

The Savior, then, was the mythic center which carried the insoluble problems of thought, society, and discipline. It was his figure which carried the tension between history and myth. Christ was, originally, Jesus of Nazareth, an historical person. He was, throughout the entire period, spoken of as this historical person. Christians knew and perpetuated his words and deeds as recorded in the Gospels. For this synchronic introduction, it does not matter to what degree the mythic elements arose, nor from where. Nor does it matter exactly how and when the assertion of divinity grew or how the relationship of the Son to God the Father was thought of by early Christians. The model of the Savior was historical and mythic; he was a Jewish Rabbi and the incarnate God.

But the Savior model contained another unification of components. From the earliest times, he was a person. He was born and he was crucified, as the Creed maintained, under Pontius Pilate. The Savior was placed in a specific time of history in the Roman Empire; it was during the reign of Tiberius. But the Savior was also spoken of in impersonal terms. He was Word; he was Spirit; he was Light. None of these words partakes of the personal . Likewise with Truth and with Way. The Savior was thus perceived both as a person and as an abstraction. As people talked about him, they had two alternatives: either that of historical reenactment (telling the story of the Gospel, repeating, exegeting, and reliving the historical deeds) or of theological reduction (seeing their Savior as a model of the mind or a symbol of value and meaning).

In an extraordinary fashion, icon and idea come together in the model of the ancient Christian Savior. I am still speaking of the "icon of the mind," the mental image, the visual model. "I am the light of the world." A person says these words; but light does not speak. When the Christians heard these words, they heard them spoken; hence they tied their vision of "light" to their vision of the person using the word "light."

As we try to understand this duality between icon and idea in the Savior, we are dealing with a phenomenon which is related to art, that is, to visual imagination. It is the nature of art that it cannot be separated into form and content. If it is separated into these two components, it ceases to be art. The Savior model belongs to the world of art because it combined discordant elements and shaped these elements into a vision. The Savior of the Gospel of John, of Ignatius, of the Gospel of Truth, of the Christian liturgy, and of the earliest hymns, was both theologacal content and linguistic shape.

And here lies one more problem of the ancient Christian understanding of salvation; it is the problem of the relation between the "Savior" as theological truth and as artistic form. The problem becomes acute in the early Christian iconoclastic dilemma. Tertullian did not want art because it might lead to idolatry. Canon 36 of Elvira did not want pictures on the walls of Spanish churches. Eusebius of Caesarea demurred from Constantine's request to send him a picture of Christ. The iconic problem in the ancient church had many roots, including the Hebraic tradition which inveighed against images and the Graeco-Roman philosophical tradition which held art in contempt. Whatever the reason, Christianity was caught in a dilemma as serious as that between myth and history:

from Elvira to the iconoclastic controversies of later times, people demanded pictures of Christ, although many Christian leaders disapproved. In fact, the very model of a "Savior" or of the "Son of Man" or of the "risen Lord" was a mental picture, a vision, an icon of language. We do not have sufficient evidence about the first two centuries of the Christian era, but we do know that, despite Tertullian's polemic in De idololatria, pictures were created (e.g., the church of Dura Europos, and the Good Shepherd in the Lateran Museum). We also know that, canon 36 of Elvira notwithstanding, the Constantinian age also produced pictures. That there were prohibitions against the making of pictures indicates that the practice was wide-spread, and from the illustrations in the catacombs onwards, a rich iconographic tradition evolves.

It is to this tradition that we must turn because it throws some light on the problems we have been discussing. Visual iconic art expressed the same salvation-perdition alternative as found in the texts we have been examining. On an ivory in the British Museum the betrayal of Peter is displayed alongside a representation of Christ carrying the cross, and next to the crucified Christ is betrayed the traitor Judas hanged. In the sarcophagus of St. Peter's Grotto, Jesus curses the fig tree and heals the woman with the issue of blood. In the mosaic of Apollinare Nuovo, Christ separated the sheep from the goats. This last model, repeated in countless variations from the Church of Torcello to the Sistine Chapel, puts before the Christian the vision of damnation and salvation, a vision out of which the entire salvatory schema grew and to which it addressed itself.

Visual iconic art also takes on the great dichotomies to which we have pointed. Polycarp, for instance, spoke of Christ as both King and Lamb (Mart. Pol. 9.3). Iconographically this polarity can be seen everywhere. The Savior figure is portrayed as Pantocrator, the figure of imperial might, of divinity, with a halo, the Eastern symbol of political power. But he is also portrayed as Lamb, the sumbol of vulnerability, of suffering and sacrifice. The iconic world takes these two symbols--victory and defeat,

167

power and suffering--and creates out of them an order
of its own. In the cupola of San Vitale, the Lamb is
carried by four angels. It becomes a cosmic entity.
Close by, on the side wall, we find the priest-king,
Melchisedek, with sacrificial symbols. The sacrifice
is cosmic; power is sacrificial. The order of art creates a relation between the two. The icon arose out of
two sides of Christian experience. To be sure, the
iconographic trend was toward power. Icons served the
clerical, priestly structure of the church. There is a
great distance between the Rabbi of Mark and the Pantocrator of Ravenna, and between the two lies the emergence of the church as a world power. But the Savior
still stands at the center.

This process is not portrayed only in Ravenna,
built when the dynamic of Christianity had shifted toward the Byzantine empire. In the catacomb of Pris-
cilla, salvation is represented (in good diaspora tradition) as the icon of the three men in the fiery fur-
nace. In the catacomb of Domitilla, Christ appears as
a person. Sarcophagi show at times symbolic salvation
(as in the many Jonah specimens at Santa Maria Anti-
qua) and at times they portray the Savior himself (as
in the Vatican Grotto). Santa Maria Maggiore depicts,
in the nave, the sequence of old Israel, surely with
some soteriological goal in mind; and in the apse is
seen the story of the birth and youth of Jesus. Between the nave and apse, the church creates a visual space
for the Christian. The tension, of course is not
merely one of iconic art; it goes back to the very
beginnings of Christianity. Paul spoke of Christ as
an historical figure; he also spoke of him in terms
of Old Testament models, of Abraham and Adam.

The Savior model, for all its many divergent
trends, is at the center of the salvation schema. The
Savior is youth (the Epiphany sarcophagi and the mo-
saics of Ravenna) and baptized youth (the baptistries
of Ravenna); the Savior is also adult and Pantocrator; he is Teacher (Pudenziana) and law-giver (Mauso-
leum of Constantia). In the orthodox baptistery of
Ravenna, the polarity is between the baptized Jesus
and, below, the adult apostles. And beneath the apostles is the empty throne; and on the throne, a folded

168

gown. Baptism is seen as an event of the past; the empty throne points to the future. The baptized wears no clothes; the purple gown is not worn. Such images portray the polarity between youth and age, between past and future; they hint at vulnerability (nakedness) and at power (the imperial robe). The church itself has a double past; one indicated by the apostles, the other by the baptismal christological scene.

And that baptismal scene also points to the issue of paganism in ancient Christianity. Beside the baptized stands not only John the Baptizer but also the river god, Jordan. The icon takes along the pagan past, just as in earlier figures Orphic elements had been incorporated into representations of Christ (as in the Ostia sarcophagus and the Aquielja mosaic). The iconic problem was not that much different, then, from the linguistic one in which pagan elements were similarly incorporated into Christian speech. In all these variations of the ancient Christian salvation complex, one model stands in the center of both language and vision, of society and cult, of ideology and art. This model was a multisema. It was the code for a broad range of experiences, desires, ideas, and social structures. It was expressed in words and in visual shapes; it had both a personal and a communal meaning; it created order.

But it also destroyed order. In Corinth, Paul protested bitterly that the Gospel of Jesus Christ which he had preached led, ironically, to schism. Apollo, Cephas, Paul and Christ became competitors. By the time of Athanasius, and even more so with Nestorius and Cyril, the model of Christ was operative in the disruption or breaking up of Christian community. Christ was at once a model for unity and disunity. In that respect, the age of Chalcedon was not that different from the time of Paul. What changed was merely a shift in emphasis, the result of numerical growth and of political success. On one level, external perdition had been conquered as the Graeco-Roman cosmos became Christian. But, on another level, it was a Pyrrhic victory. Schism became more pervasive; Jerome, Cyril and Augustine were as anxious about salvation as Paul, Ignatius, and Clement of Rome had been. When, by the time of Constantine, the persecuted became the persecutors, the political potential in the salvation schema emerged in full force.

The Savior model revealed and supported both the extraordinary ambiguity as well as the dynamic of ancient Christianity. It could serve clashing groups simultaneously: the baptismal scene in the Arian and Orthodox Baptisteries of Ravenna are, iconically, identical. The Savior model could support political resistance as well as rebellion: Christ is our Imperator, said the martyrs of Scilli to the Roman Court. The model could support autocratic power: Constantine himself placed the tombs of the apostles around him, a final display of imperial might. The model could lead as easily to political adjustment as to pacific subordination. It could be the patron of culture and at the same time support counter-culture. Christianity grew, in effect, within a primal tension between religion as a canopy for the status quo and religion as a tool and platform for social and intellectual change. The icon-model-myth of the Savior was, as were the texts we examined earlier, a perfect example for that conflict.

Samuel Laeuchli

170

RETURN TO THE DIVINE:

SALVATION IN THE THOUGHT OF PLOTINUS AND ORIGEN[1]

In the third century it was Plotinus and Origen
whose anthropologies were to have an important and lasting influence upon the thought of succeeding theologians
and philosophers. Their views were formative also for
the mysticism, both pagan and Christian, which was to
be developed in subsequent generations. In particular,
Origen's ascetic concepts and mystical perception of the
human soul pervaded the thought of later thinkers in
the East as well as in the West; they are an impressive
contribution to the progressive understanding of human
salvation. Fundamental to the thought of both Plotinus
and Origen is their insistence on the divine origin and
divine nature of the individual human soul. Their major
concern, indeed the goal of their thought, was the ultimate "return" of the soul, by means of knowledge, to
unity with its divine source. Both were convinced that
the human soul belongs to the world of intelligible
reality, and both undertook to describe, each in his
own way, the means by which this union with Reality
could be attained.
    Origen and Plotinus were products of the ecclec-
tic intellectual environment of the Egyptian metropolis
of Alexandria. They both shared the Platonic tradition
as this had developed by the third century. It is believed that each attended, though at different times,
the lectures of Ammonius Saccas, a key figure in the
establishment of Neoplatonism. Although both men shared
a common tradition, it manifested itself in their writings in different ways. Plotinus, a pagan, recast Platonic ideas into a new pattern of thought. Origen, a
defender of Christianity, adopted Platonic views as
these could be called into service to help explain the
Christian understanding of God, of human nature, and of
human destiny. These Platonic views he revised and reshaped to as to make them congruent with Christian beliefs. Thus, although their concepts are in many ways

similar, the significant differences between Origen and Plotinus stem from their religious orientation. The purpose of this essay, then, is to present a brief analysis and comparison of the understanding of salvation in the thought of Plotinus and Origen with a view to determining the sources behind their similarities as well as their differences.

Both Plotinus and Origen believed that the rational soul participates in the divine eternal world and that its origin lies outside of time in the realm of the "intelligible" or divine.[2] However, there is a difference in how each perceives the status of the soul as it participates in the divine, that is, the nature of the soul's participation in its transcendent source. According to Plotinus, the human rational soul, which is a person's true nature, is a direct emanation of the divine essence. It is a part of the divine world, a being which exists on the lowest level of divinity and therefore in continuous and direct relationship with the divine intellect.[3] Origen, as a Christian who was influenced by the biblical view of creation, could not accept so exalted a view of human nature, that the rational soul was a part of the divine and in direct association with it. This biblical pessimism notwithstanding, he did find, through a rational interpretation of the Genesis narratives, the basis for a qualified assertion of the soul's participation in the divine.

According to Origen, the rational soul is a created being; created outside of time, it is nevertheless created. For this reason, it is unstable, subject to change and alteration,[4] in contradistinction to the simple and eternally changeless essence of uncreated divinity.[5] Therefore, the human soul is not of the same essence as the divine,[6] but is capable of sharing or participating in the divine.[7] Referring to the biblical account of creation, Origen states that it is the rational soul which was created in the "image" of God.[8] It is capable, accordingly, of perceiving and understanding, if it so wills, the intelligible divine truth and, through its imitation of the divine Logos, is capable of attaining perfection and "likeness" to God.[9] It is through this interpretation of the imago Dei that

Origen, like Plotinus, can speak of the soul's participation in its divine source. Yet it is his adherence to the biblical view of creation that causes him to differ both from Plotinus and the other Platonists of his time. A Platonic concept has been modified in order to make it congruent with Christian belief.

Plotinus believed that in their original state all souls were pure rational beings, logoi or logika, alike and equal in their contemplation of the divine intellect and in perfect communion with it.[10] However, these rational beings turned away from their contemplation of the Good and assumed material bodies. The "fall" of the rational beings is considered by both Plotinus and Origen as a consequence of this turning away. For Plotinus, this "fall" was both a cosmological necessity and an indication of the soul's voluntary inclination towards that which is void and vain. The embodiment of the rational soul is necessary for its own development and for the subsequent creation and perfection of the cosmos. But still it is a "fall," a voluntary self-alienation of the soul from the Good.[11] Plotinus never reconciles the "necessary" and "voluntary" elements of the logoi's turning away from their original state.[12] Origen, on the other hand, attributes the fall of souls to their created, generated nature. By virtue of the fact that they once did not exist and then came into existence, rational souls were necessarily subject to change and alteration; inherent instability is part of their nature.[13] It was this instability which led the souls, albeit created in the image of God, to make a wrong choice, to neglect God, and thus to fall away from God and into evil. So Origen, although believing the fall to be an unavoidable consequence of genetic instability, nevertheless holds these created beings morally responsible for their fall.[14] However, in spite of the logika's estrangement from God, they still retain their participation in the divine essence and thus have the ability, potentially, to return to their original pristine state.

Adhering to the Platonic doctrine of "assimilation to God," both Plotinus and Origen maintain that the world of sense is alien to the soul and a hindrance to the soul's realization of its own true nature. Each believes that a person's goal should be to become liberated from the things of sense and to realize one's divine nature as <u>logos</u> or <u>logikos</u>, thus regaining one's original status. The rational soul possesses within itself both the desire and power for communion with the divine. The attainment of perfection and the regaining of original purity is thus within the grasp of human capability.[15]

According to Plotinus, the rational or "higher" soul remains always in the intelligible world, in continuous and direct contemplation of intelligible realities.[16] It remains eternally stable and impassible, untouched by the passions, sin and suffering which are a part of the sensible world.[17] Eternally maintained in the intelligible universe, and in constant communion with the One, the rational soul continually receives from the One, through the eternal and spontaneous emanation of its energy, the power always to return to the world of the intellect. In its process of creative emanation, the One gives movement to the soul and the power to return to its source.[18] It is thus the continuous illumination of the soul by the One which provides the soul both with the desire for, and the power necessary to achieve, salvation. A person needs only to turn inward to recognize this impulse the power within and to pursue the necessary moral and intellectual discipline involved in the process of purification.[19] Through moral training, philosophical reflection, and the study of the sciences, the soul gradually attains knowledge of the Good and ascends thereby to the intelligible world.[20] Thus, in Plotinus' view, there is no need for what might be called additional, special or providential grace to assist the soul, nor any need for the mediation of prayer, for rites or sacraments. Within human nature itself exists all that is required for the process towards salvation, a process culminating in the soul's ascent towards purification and the final appearance or vision of the One. It is this conscious awareness within the soul of the divine presence which allows for the soul's ultimate awakening and realization of its true nature.[21] In spite of this universal possibility, however, not all are capable of reaching the highest level, for few are aware of

the power within themselves, and still fewer are willing
to undertake the vigorous intellectual and moral discipline necessary to bring the true divine nature of the
soul to full realization. It is for this reason that
those who do experience the divine vision are few, and
their experience of it is rare.[22] Yet it is still true
that the vision or appearance of the One does come
naturally to anyone who is properly prepared to receive it.[23] This is both similar to and, in some respects, divergent from Origen's view in which he maintains that it requires persistent and steady effort, in
addition to God's continuous grace and guidance, for the
soul to regain its original state of purity.

Origen, too, as we have already seen, believed
that the rational soul is capable of participating in
the divine life. As the "image" of God, or of the
divine Wisdom, the soul is able, if it wills, to perceive and understand the divine intelligible verities.[24]
However, Origen could not, as a Christian, accept the
idea that a person's true self (rational soul) is by
nature eternally pure, stable, changeless, and impassible. Origen believed that it was the whole soul which
had fallen in its entirety and was therefore, all of it,
in need of purification. It is the entire soul which,
because created, is mutable, provisional, incomplete,
and dependent. All that the soul possesses is due to
God's power or will, and it requires God's constant
and continuous grace for its spiritual status as well
as for its very existence. This assertion of the soul's
unstable nature and of its dependence upon God's grace
is of primary significance to Origen's discussion of
the soul's spiritual ascent.[25] Unlike Plotinus' description of the "rational" soul, for Origen there is
no part of the soul (rational or otherwise) which inherently possesses goodness. Rather, the soul is given
a share in goodness by God's grace in accordance with
its developing capacity to receive it.

Both Origen and Plotinus claim that the ability
and power, movement and desire, to return to God have
from the beginning been implanted by God within the
soul.[26] Both Origen and Plotinus state that it is the
responsibility of the individual soul to recognize the
power within it and, by means of this power, to strive

conscientiously to attain the world of intellible realities.[27] But it is only Origen, who holds to the soul's
unstable and changeable nature, in whose writings we
find the insistence on the soul's inability, of itself,
to realize and utilize the divine power implanted within it to attain ultimate communion with God. It is important for the soul to realize and acknowledge its
own limitations, that is, its instability and dependence,
if it is to turn to God for that grace without which
salvation is impossible.[28] When it does this, the soul
begins to receive God's guidance, those personal and
individual acts of grace which guide it through the
various phases of the ascent towards God, all in accordance with the given soul's maturity and capacity
for spiritual progress.[29]. It is through the soul's con-
scientious effort, its imitation of the divine Logos,
and with the help and guidance of the Logos, that the
soul is capable of being perfected and led to union
with God. It is the Logos which provides the soul
first with the moral power with which it can do battle
against sin, and then with an increase of intellectual
insight as it advances towards God, during which ad-
vance it begins to perceive and understand those mystical divine truths which heretofore had been hidden from
it.[30]

For Origen, God reveals himself by means of the
Logos both in history and in the inner life of the individual. God reveals himself through the Holy Scrip-
tures and to each individual in accordance with that
individual's capacity to receive him.[31] Thus, unlike
Plotinus, Origen maintains that salvation is univer-
sally available to all, not just to those who are intellectually capable.[32] The means of salvation are in
accordance with an individual's needs or degree of
insight at a given moment, but salvation itself is
potentially available to all.

Although the process by which an individual
soul attains true knowledge is described differently
by Plotinus and Origen, each sees the ultimate goal
as the same: The soul's mystical union with the divine.
Each describes the relationship of the soul to the
divine in terms of a mystical marriage, making use of
the Platonic myth of Eros and Psyche as elaborated in

the Symposium.[33] After much searching and longing for the Good, the soul is joined to the Good in a union which both Plotinus and Origen see as analogous to the union of earthly lovers.[34] But the union of the soul with the Good in no way partakes of the sensual; rather, it is that fulfillment by which the soul, in perfect self-knowledge, comprehends the eternal divine realities. This is the goal of human existence, the end of life's journey.[35] Plotinus sees the last stage of this journey as the complete union of the soul with the One, a state in which the soul has turned completely inward, where pleasures and happiness are from within, when the soul has been freed from everything alien and external. Things of sense have become relegated to the level of meaningless accessories, and the soul itself has become one, both with itself and with the divine.[36] Plotinus does not say that the soul becomes "identical" with the divine; rather, the soul has finally realized its own true divine nature and has thereby been completely fulfilled by the One.[37] It is even possible, Plotinus claims, for this state of unification to be attained by a purified soul while still in the earthly body, but such experiences are very rare and of brief duration. Final and permanent union with the One is possible only after death, when the soul is completely free of the body.[38]

In language similar to Plotinus', Origen describes the final union of the soul with God as that stage in which the soul will no longer be conscious of anything other than God; it will think God and hold God and God will be the mode and measure of its every movement. God will be all in all to the soul.[39] But nowhere does Origen speak of a oneness or unity of the soul with the divine while still in an earthly body. The soul can indeed reach that contemplative stage in which there is an awareness of the divine and an approach of the divine towards the soul, but this awareness and approach stops short of complete oneness or union.[40] While in the earthly body, the soul is still too weak and unstable to attain complete union with God, even for a rare or brief instant. The earthly body is in fact an impediment both to the soul's complete union with God as well as to its fitness for such union.[41] Thus, according to Origen, complete and lasting union with the divine can be achieved only in the life hereafter.[42]

From a common Platonic tradition, then, there emerged two views of salvation, one of them pagan and one of them Christian. What they have in common stems from this shared tradition. Where their views differ stems from their respective understanding of human nature. Plotinus, as did the pagan Platonists, adopted certain elements of the tradition, reinterpreted them, and developed out of them an exalted anthropology. For Plotinus, the human is essentially divine; the true self, or rational soul, is a member of the intelligible universe, a stable, impassible, immortal, divine entity which is uncreated and exists from before all time, eternally sustained in the intelligible universe and in constant communion with the divine. The goal of human existence is to understand this essential divinity and, through virtue and philosophy, to restore it to its proper, original relationship to the One and to the divine world.

Origen, also a Platonist, differed from Plotinus precisely in his adaptation of a more biblically based view of creation and of the imperfection of human nature. Thus he used those Platonic concepts which could the more readily explain his Christian anthropology. Origen is less optimistic than Plotinus about the inherent goodness of human nature, but more optimistic about the possibility of eternal salvation for all created beings. Heeding the biblical accounts of creation, Origen assigns to the human soul the status of creatureliness, albeit created from all eternity in the image of God. As such, the soul has a certain "kinship" with God, is immortal, and capable of participating in the divine life. But it is not essentially divine. As created, the entire soul is basically unstable and in need of God's grace and assistance. The aim of one's life should be to purify oneself from things of sense and to return to fellowship with God. For the Christian, this is done through faith in Christ (Logos) and diligent imitation of Him who guides all souls in their return to God.

Antonia Tripolitis

SOTERIOLOGICAL COMMONPLACES IN CYRIL OF ALEXANDRIA'S
COMMENTARY ON THE GOSPEL OF JOHN

In his Commentary on John, Cyril of Alexandria employs a large number of images and formulae when speaking of salvation. The reader finds the expected concentration upon the saving virtue of the incarnation, but other strands are important as well. Often emphasis will shift to some other aspect of Christ's life, his death, or his resurrection and ascension. Sometimes a moral strand issuing from Christ's example, or the gift of the Holy Spirit will predominate.

Cyril states that flesh is made incorruptible through its assumption by the Godhead (6.48-50).[1] Yet he can contend equally that faith is the door to incorruption (6.47). Death is conquered by Christ's death (13.36), by his resurrection (12.24), by his incarnation (8129), and finally in some wise by Christ's teaching (6.68). Closely allied with victory over death and corruption is the overcoming of sin in the flesh (14.20). The devil is defeated, both by Christ's coming (8.56) and by his death (6.38-39). In one passage, Cyril says that this defeat frees men from error, gives light to those in darkness, and liberates them from the devil's snares (12.27-8), while on the very next page Cyril turns about and ennumerates three quite different benefits derived from the same victory: the end of death, the destruction of corruption, and freedom from the "ancient curse" (12.27-8). The tyranny of passions is quelled by the incarnation (3.5), by the eucharist (6.56), or by following Christ's moral example (12.27-8). Cyril pictures redemption as manumission: we are set free from the bondage of flesh and sin (8.34), having been ransomed by Christ's love (8.21), for only Christ, who is free by nature, can give freedom to others (8.35). Cyril also pictures redemption as Christ's vicarious suffering of the penalty due for our sins (13.31-2).

Through Christ, mankind is returned to its prelapsarian state (7.39), and the image of God is renewed (1.32-3). Cyril is not content, however, with a simple restoration of fallen humanity, for he states that we attain a new condition above and beyond the limits of our nature (12.27-8). Through the humanity we share with the incarnate Christ, we are received into sonship (10.14-5), and raised up to God's level, which was previously alien to us (1.13). Again, through that common humanity, we share in Christ's resurrection (6.51), and are ascended with him to the Father (13.36). This physical aspect of filiation is paralleled by a spiritual and moral one as well. In one passage, Cyril equates filiation with spiritual regeneration (1.13), while, in another, he asserts that if one would be a son of God, he must love Christ (8.42), or, again elsewhere, he must conform his will to that of God (8.37).

Cyril is especially fond of the figure of Jesus as a teacher and illuminator, whether as moral guide (13.17-7), or as instructor who dispenses saving knowledge (10.16), banishes darkness (9.6-7) and the errors of polytheism (1.10). Christ is the source of a divine illumination which is distinct from teaching (1.9), likened rather to creation, a spontaneous giving by God (1.9).

Certainly, among these images, Cyril has favorites, such as sonship and the transformation from corruption to incorruption, both with their strong Pauline overtones; none the less, he ranges wide enough to forbid allying himself with any particular, dominant typology. Almost the entire spectrum of expressions for salvation current in the vocabulary of Cyril's time is plentifully represented in his Commentary on John. An interesting exception is Cyril's customary reluctance to speak of our salvation as a vision of God. Yet, when discussing John 14.21, he does identify eternal bliss with the perfect vision of God, compelled, no doubt, by the verse under consideration (14.21). While Cyril may very well have found the vision of God a temperamentally uncongenial expression, it is tempting as well to suppose that he may have shied away from a figure so closely associated with the tradition of spiritual theology stemming from Origen.[2]

Cyril's soteriological vocabulary is not simply

extensive; it is conservative as well, and he manages it with great flexibility and terseness. Relying upon a community of discourse for which this was the common coin, he can assume, apparently, that the values he attaches to these terms and images are known by his audience and accepted by them. For example, when Cyril says that "Christ transfers the glory of adoption through himself to all the race" (12.2-3), and says it without further explanation, he must assume that the apparatus of the physical theory of the atonement, participation and filiation, were familiar enough to his readers that they could fill in, as it were, the archbishop's shorthand.

Indeed, when discussing salvation, Cyril seldom makes what we would consider to be explanations. Generally he seems disinclined to tie himself down to any sequential argument or model which might claim to demonstrate precisely how a particular blessing must be the product of a particular aspect of the Redeemer's life and work, or how it is to be appropriated by those who receive it. On one of the rare occasions when Cyril does offer just such an explanation, he brings it up only to reject it. Furthermore, he rejects it, significantly, as neither suitable nor necessary (14.20). Rarely will he expand upon the implications of a soteriological image or statement. His custom, instead, is to make short, positive, dogmatic assertions: ". . . the death of all has been undone in Christ's death, and the power of corruption brought to an end . . ." (8.51). "For Christ coming to dwell with us, lulls the law which rages in the flesh . . ." (6.56). We "are made partakers of the divine nature by the gift of the Holy Spirit" (14.4). Many of these brief statements are the ghosts of past arguments and explanations, produced by other minds in other circumstances. The motivating force behind their origin is spent. They have become, for Cyril, elements in a stable theological vocabulary.

For all of Cyril's disinclination to provide elaborated arguments, he still does present extended soteriological passages in which clusters of his characteristically brief assertions are grouped in a variety of ways. Some of these clusters are shaped for rhetorical effect. Cyril was strongly influenced by his reading of Paul's letters. Beyond matters of theology, Cyril's writing is full of echoes of Paul's literary style. He shares with the Apostle a taste for series of balanced antitheses. Speaking, for instance, of the Word as _life_, he writes:

> He rather raises (to life), he does not fall (into death). He abolishes death, but is not subject to corruption. He gives life to what lacks life, but does not seek life from another. Even as light cannot become darkness, so it is impossible for life to cease to be life . . . .

He died as man, but rose as God (12.24). Here the ideas associate easily with the image of Christ as _life_, and the grouping seems as natural as it is effective. Elsewhere, speaking of salvation as transformation, Cyril ranges more widely: Christ effects a change from death to life, from corruption to incorruption, from love of earthly things to desire to please God, from slavery to sonship, from earth to the city above, from sin to righteousness, from impurity of human nature to sanctification by the Holy Spirit, from dishonor to honor, ignorance to knowledge, cowardice to endurance (14.31). Although heterogeneous, these ten elements are tied together at least by the concept of change.

Often, however, such a unifying focus is missing. Consequently, the groupings may easily appear to be negligent compilations of _idées recues_ with neither shape nor theological purpose. To take an example, Cyril joins together five different strands in one short passage. Christ calls us (a) to eternal life, (b) to forgiveness of sins, (c) to shedding death and corruption, (d) to righteousness and glory, and (e) to boasting in the sonship of God (8.25). Similarly, when commenting upon John 3.17, Cyril groups together loving kindness, freedom from bondage, transformation of the law, release from sin, and healing of the world's infirmity (loc. cit.).

The facility with which Cyril marshalls these varied images, as well as the wide repertory which he deploys in the course of his commentary, including his

reluctance to develop them in any systematic fashion--
all these suggest that some particular bias must have
informed his thinking. Any reconstruction of that habit
of mind is necessarily speculative, but there are certain
indicators which may perhaps be profitably combined.

While Cyril is not ordinarily particularly self-
conscious, theologically, he is articulately concerned
about the propriety and adequacy of theological language. Principally he distrusts any attempt to frame
ideas of God's transcendent glory and divinity:

> Who among men would not be convinced that
> our human faculties cannot supply either
> words or ideas through which he might ex-
> press, in an irreproachable and infallible
> manner, the peculiar attributes of the di-
> vine and ineffable nature? Consequently he
> must depend upon the words of which he is
> capable as a means to express what surpasses
> his understanding. How, indeed, is it possi-
> ble to express something clearly which tran-
> scends the limits of our comprehension?
> (13.21)

Cyril applies implications of this reserve to other aspects of theology as well. He says, for example, that
"experience is more powerful than language to convince
and satisfy" (14.21), and, in one instance, he expresses this scruple with explicit reference to the aim of
the incarnation, that is, our salvation (14.20). In the
light of this position, Cyril's reluctance to provide
extensive systematic treatment of issues is quite understandable. It is easy to imagine that he could have
felt that it would be misleading to invest heavily in
any particular image or to integrate any image so
tightly into a larger theological framework that the
reader would be left with the impression that Cyril,
or anyone else, could claim to plumb the divine mystery
and reveal its inner logic.

For all the force of these reservations, Cyril
of course continues to use theological language. However powerless it may be to explicate the mysteries of
faith, it still serves a useful function, for it can

at least point to that which ultimately eludes it. One might go further and suggest that, while each of the images and terms which make up Cyril's soteriological armory names a reality lying beyond its grasp, the response which the individual terms evoke highlights only a limited facet of that reality. Considering then their individual inadequacy to make more than a partial assertion of Christ's work, Cyril's preference for a large and varied collection of images, as well as his custom of presenting them in clusters, becomes less puzzling. The language with which Cyril works might be seen to form a sort of continuum within which there are closer and remoter links, a set of predicates, always approximate, of an ineffable subject. Such a spectrum seems to have been taken so much for granted by Cyril that he can use a single image as a cipher to stand, as the context plainly demands, for the full realtiy of salvation (e.g., 12.23).

In just the same way that Cyril will apply a particular term or group of terms to the work of Christ, he will, on occasion, make the general observation that Christ is the source of "all that is fairest," or of "all good things." For Cyril, such a generality is not simply collective, but points as well to a basic unity of salvation, prior to the divisions and false distinctions introduced by our partial and approximate terminology. Theological language, for Cyril, is the product of a world which has experienced the scattering of the fall. Scripture alone appears exempt, in part, from this limitation. The unity of Christ's saving activity has been refracted by the complexity of our experience into various discreet images answering to our own personal needs. In one instance, when speaking of the union of the Father and the Son, Cyril states that the blessings conferred by Christ proceed "from a single common munificence." If there is a single source of blessings, the bestowal of them can be seen as a single action. In treating of John 16.7, Cyril provides an elaborately arresting picture of Christ's career as a saving drama, sweeping from the incarnation through the resurrection and ascension to the dispensation of the Holy Spirit (loc. cit.).

Cyril does divide this narrative into phases and assigns appropriate works to each phase, but, as he piles commonplace upon commonplace, the distinctions between the particular effects of Christ's work become blurred and the impression of unity of activity based upon the skeletal structure of history is intensified. The predication of blessings to a precise moment in the life of Jesus is secondary. Just as Cyril will allow himself the convenient distinctions of two nature exegesis, while insisting at the same time on the actual indissoluble union of the incarnation, it is reasonable to assume that the divisions and distinctions which he makes here are largely a similar accomodation of habits of theological discourse but do not seriously compromise a basic view that it is the entire drama of Christ, rather than any particular aspect, which is the vehicle of redemption.

These contentions should help clarify the position which allowed for Cyril's theological procedures, with its peculiarities. Even if the work of salvation is coterminous with the oeconomia and forms one seamless whole, it is a phenomenon which can be intuited only faintly by the mind and which is basically inacessible to language. Religious discourse must confine itself to a second level, describing the phenomenon in terms of its manifest effects, already conditioned by human perception with its variety and limits. Cyril appears to have felt that these limitations denied the possibility of constructing a definitive description of Christ's work. Some, among his soteroological formulae, do fall easily into a pattern; some do not. But in so far as they all point, without misleading, to Christ and his work, they are, for the archbishop, acceptable and harmonious articulations of the faith.

Joseph Lee McInerney

OUR LOSS

We have lost a colleague --
    discerning, fair, involved,
        brooking no nonsense --
    a citizen of conscience and principle
    who deserved and received our respect.

They have lost a teacher --
    conscientious, demanding, concerned,
        insistent on quality fare --
    an academic giant of disciplined brilliance.

All have lost an artist --
    dealing in music's magic·of ordered
    harmonies, of reasoned sound --
        a soul that sense and searched and
        loved
    another level of our landlocked lot.

And you have lost a husband,
    you a father,
        to you he was a son,
        to you a neighbor --
    not perfect, neither claiming to be so;
    intense, not always able to be as human
        as he might have wished --
    oft embattled by the gulf between abstract
    principles and overpow'ring realities.

But I have lost a friend --
    something he never said he was to me
        (nor did I ever say the same to him);
    something he did not need to say,
        whether or not we agreed on other things,
    because he was -- we were --
        and that sufficed.

ROBERT FRANKLIN EVANS (Kraft and Harvey)

1. Van A. Harvey joined the Penn faculty in 1968;
Robert A. Kraft came in 1963. Most of the quotations
used in this essay are taken from departmental files.

2. This and the next quotation are taken from the
Chairman's recommendation to the College Dean, Spring,
1962.

3. Of Evans' competence in philosophy of religion,
a colleague noted: "Evans is fully familiar with current work in this field. . . (He displays) outstanding
critical and expository skills. . . . ability to debate points which are not at the heart of contemporary problems and . . . (an) active grasp of the philosophical complexities" (May 1967).

4. In a letter dated 27 July 1961, Evans expressed
some of his feelings on this matter: "I do not want to
appear trivial, but of course the charge of triviality
could be levelled at either or both sides in the case
of a dispute over this matter. I have stronger personal feelings on this than do many Episcopal clergy,
and I certainly would be most uncomfortable if it were
assumed by anyone in authority that I would and should
not wear clerical garb. There was some embarassment
about this when I first came here (to Western Michigan
University), and the final understanding reached with
the administration was that they would definitely pre-
fer it that I not wear clerical garb, but that they
would not object if I did."

5. These quotations from students are taken from the
annual student course guides published at Penn.

6. Evans' sentiments are clear in a letter of February 1967: "If I am not officially notified this spring
of my promotion, I shall interpret this as a signal to
revive my long lapsed efforts to find a post elsewhere.
If I am successful in securing an offer elsewhere, and
if I am then offered promotion here, this will surely
be evidence contributing to the thesis that the university tends to promote a man only when its hand is

forced by virtue of rival offers."

***

THE EXEGESIS OF I JOHN 3.19-20 (Richardson)

1. Handbuch zum N.T.: Die Katholischen Briefe, Vol. 4, Pt. 2 (Tübingen, 1911), p. 122. "Since verse 17 contains a demand for sharpening the conscience, an interpretation of tranquilizing it in verse 19 would be very out of place. Hence one could insert an οὐ between αὐτοῦ and πείσομεν and delete the words ὅτι ἐὰν καταγ. ἡμ. ἡ κ.as a scribal insertion due to verse 21. Then we would have a very appropriate warning to those without conscience, of the God who searches the heart. But the best thing is surely to abide by the assertion that the text is corrupt." Translations throughout are my own unless otherwise noted.

2. The Johannine Epistles (Moffat N.T. Comm.) (New York, 1946), p. 87.

3. Adumbrationes in Epistolas canonicas, Griech. Christ. Schriftst. ed. o. Stählin (Leipzig, 1909), Vol. 3, p. 214. "'Because,' he says, 'God is greater than our heart,' that is, (he refers to) conscience, a divine power which is closely attendant on the soul; hence he adds, 'he (it?) knows all.'" The understanding of 'heart' as 'conscience' in 20b is dependent upon rendering 20a as "our heart condemns us."

4. Q. S. F. Tertulliani, De Anima, ed. J. Waszink (Amsterdam, 1947), 15.4, p. 19: "and John says each man is condemned by his own heart." This comes in a scriptural catena to show that mind and vital power have their seats in the heart. For the date of the De anima, see ibid., p. 6.

5. A rare exception to this is J. Bonsirven, Epîtres de Saint Jean (Verbum Salutis IX) (Paris, 1954), p. 172. He renders thus: It is in this that we will know we are of the truth, and that we will reassure our heart before Him, namely that, if our heart brings any accusation against us, God is greater than our heart and knows all things." This involves suppressing the ὅτι before μείζων, and viewing "know we are of the truth: and "reassure our heart before Him" as involving a single idea:

viz. being "at peace with God" (p. 176). It is an absolute act of abandon to God, not by relying on our own merits, that we achieve this peace (p. 176). The basic "ecumenical interpretation" is thus reached by a different grammatical route.

6. Commentaire de la première Epître de S. Jean, text and tr. Paul Agaësse (Sources chrétiennes) (Paris, 1961), p. 280, Tractate VI.3.

7. R. Schnackenburg, Die Johannesbriefe, 3rd ed. Freiburg, 1965), ad loc.

8. R. Bultmann, Die drei Johannesbriefe (Meyer Comm. XIV) (Göttingen, 1967), ad loc.

9. This is, however, the exegesis of Uttendoerfer in his article, "Ein Kennzeichen dafür, dass wir aus der Wahrheit sind," in Neue Kirchliche Zeitschrift, Vol. 11 (1900), pp. 955-1002.

10. A. E. Brooke, The Johannine Epistles (ICC) (New York, 1912; (repr. 1928), p. 98.

11. Biblia Novi Testamenti Illustrata, Vol. 2 (Dresden, 1719), p. 1638.

12. "Glossen sum ersten Johannesbrief III" in Neue Kirchliche Zeitschrift. Vol. 13 (1902), pp. 632-645.

13. Commentarii: in Epistolas canonicas, Vol. 10 (Antwerp, 1681), p. 480b-481a.

14. Johannes Lorinus, In Catholicas tres B. Johannis . . . Commentarii (Lyons, 1609), p. 91b.

15. See F. Stegmuller, Repertorium biblicum medii aevi (Madrid 1950-62), Vol. 4, items 5806-5808, pp. 45-47. I am much indebted to the same author's medieval list prepared for Schnackenburg, op. cit., pp. xiv-xv.

16. Thomas Aquinas, Opera Omnia (Rome, 1570). Also Parmia ed., 1869, Vol. 23. It is not in the Venice ed. of 1775.

17. Sixtus Senensis, Bibliotheca Sancta (Cologne, 1576), p. 329. The 1st ed. was Venice, 1566.

18. There are many candidates in medieval manuscripts for the appellation "Thomas Anglicus:" i.e., Thomas of York, d. 1310; Thomas of Sutton, d. 1315; Thomas Wilton, ? date; and Thomas Walleys or of Wales, d. 1340-50. The last is clearly meant by Sisto. For some attempt to straighten out the various writers called "Thomas Anglicus" see Schmaus, M., Der liber propugnatorius des Tho-

mas Anglicus (Münster, 1930), pp. 1-12.

19. See J. Quétif and J. Echard, Scriptores Ordinis Praedicatorum (Paris, 1719-21), Vol. 1, p. 6b.

20. Cornelius a Lapide, op. cit., p. 6b.

21. Nicolaus Gorranus, In Acta Apostolorum et Singulas Apostolorum . . . epistolas et Apocalypsin Commentarii (Antwerp, 1620). It was first published under Thomas Aquinas' name, Paris, 1543.

22. Op. cit., p. 151a.

23. Pseudo Walfrid Strabo, Migne, PL 114, col. 700. The ordinary glcss goes back to the early 12th century and was begun by Anselm of Léon.

24. Migne, PL 209, col. 275.

25. Opera Omnia in universum V. et N. Testamentum, Vol. 7 (Venice, 1703), p. 352a.

26. Postillae perpetuae in V. et N. Testamentum (Bibliorum Sacrorum . . . cum Glossa Ordinaria et Nicolai Lyrani Expositionibus) (Lyons, 1545), Vol. 6, p. 232, col. 4.

27. Opera Omnia (Montreuil, 1901), Vol. 14, p. 38.

28. Historia et Monumenta Joannis Hus (Nuremburg, 1715), Vol. 2, p. 338.

29. In omnes D. Pauli et aliorum Apostolorum epistolas Commentarii (Lyons), Vol. 5, p. 395d.

30. Parker Society, ed., Vol. 43, Expositions and Notes etc. by William Tyndale, ed. H. Walter (Cambridge, 1849), p. 194.

31. Franciscus Tillemans, Elucidatio in omnes Epistolas Apostolicas (Paris, 1532).

32. Benedictus Arias, Elucidationes in omnia sanctorum Apostolorum Scripta (Antwerp, 1588).

33. Johannes Ferus (1495-1554), the learned exegete and cathedral preacher of Mainz. He was accused of Lutheran sympathies and all his works were put on the Index donec corrigantur, except the commentaries on Mt., Jn. and Jn. epistles. The sermons on the latter were given in 1545, and published in Paris, 1553: In sacrosanctum J. Chr. D. N. Evangelium sec. Johannem . . . Enarrationes . . . Accessit operi eiudem Divi Johannis Epistola Prima. Item pro concione enarrata an. 1545. His exegesis (p. 547a) follows Luther's: "See here how great a good a serene and composed conscience can be! Even, he says, if our heart condemn us and remind us

of our past sins, nevertheless we know and have sure trust, because God is greater than our heart, that is, his mercy is greater than all our sins, and the merit of Christ outweighs our transgression.

34. Although Luther's lectures were not published until 1709, his exegesis became widely known. Henry Bullinger (although he rejects it) knew it by 1537; see In Omnes Apostolicas Epistolas . . . Commentarii (Zürich 1537), p. 95. Matthais Flacius' version of it appeared in 1570 (see below). It does not, however, seem to have been known by Tyndale (1531) or Oecolampadius, In Epistolam Johannis apostoli catholicam primam (Nuremberg, 1524), pp. 60-1.

35. Commentarii (Köln, 1615), Vol. 16, p. 273.

36. I regret that I have been unable to discover the source whence Lorinus drew his knowledge of the wider and positive interpretation of our text. He gives both the quotation from Cain (Gen. 4.13) and one from 1 Ki. 4.29. These are lacking in Luther, Bullinger, John Wild, Flacius, Salmeron and Hunnius. A close examination of Salmeron's text shows his dependence upon John Wild and Bullinger. Whether Lorinus has a Catholic or Protestant source, I cannot say; but the fact that all three Jesuits (Salmeron, Lorinus and Cornelius) do not treat this interpretation as heretical, but merely as erroneous, a straining of the text, suggests that there were Catholics as well as Protestants who upheld it. As Lorinus gives it, the exegesis is less patently Lutheran that John Wild's. Whether this belongs to the 16th century or antedates Luther (though Luther doubtless arrived at his view quite independently) will only become clear as more late medieval materials become available.

37. Vorlesung über dem I Brief des Johannes 1527, (Weimar ed., 1898), Vol. 20, pp. 715-20. I translate from the George Rörer manuscript, which is livelier, and on our text fuller, than the more polished version of Jacob Probst, which was first published in Bremen, 1708. The Pelikan-Hanson E.T. of Luther's Works, Vol. 30, The Catholic Epistles (St. Louis, 1967), tr. of 1 John by Walter Hanson, follows the Probst version.

38. Op. cit., p. 717.

39. Ibid.

40. The Probst version reads: "Our conscience is a single droplet; but the reconciled God is a sea of comfort" (ibid., p. 716).

41. Ibid., pp. 716-8.

42. I am dependent upon G. C. F. Lücke, Commentar über die Brief des Evangelisten Johannes, 2nd ed. (Bonn, 1836; E.T. by T.G. Repp, Edinburgh, 1887), for the Greek text of Matthäi, p. 216, n. 122.

43. Gnomon Novi Testamenti (Tübingen, 1742), p. 1055.

44. "We make our hearts confident," James Murdock, The N.T. A Literal Translation from the Syriac Peshito (New York, 1851). Tremellius had rendered, "persuasum reddimus cor nostrum' (1508); see the revision by John Leusden and Charles Schaaf, Novum Testamentum Syriacum cum versione latina (Leyden, 1709).

45. Bedc, Migne, PL, Vol. 93, col. 104; Glos, órd., PL 114, col. 700.

46. Op. cit., Vol. 6, p. 232, col. 4.

47. Corp. Ref. ed., Vol. 83, Johannis Calvini Opera, Vol. 15 (1896), col. 341. (1st ed. 1551).

48. Op. cit., p. 395d.

49. Op. cit., p. 280, 282.

50. Nicene and Post-Nicene Fathers, 1st Series, Augustine, Vol. 7 (New York, 1888), Homily VI.3, p. 494.

51. Des.Erasmi Roterodami in Novum Testamentum Annotationes (Basel, 1540), p. 767.

52. Weimar ed., Die Deutsche Bibel, Vol. 7 (1931), pp. 334-5.

53. For English versions see: L. A. Weigle, The N.T. Oxtapla (New York, 1962), p. 1362, and The English Hexapla (of the N.T.) (London, 1841). For Tyndale of 1526, J. P. Dabney (ed.), The New Testament of our L. S. J. Chr. by William Tyndale (New York, 1837). The Wiclif-Purvey N.T. (between 1395 and 1408) followed the Vulgate closely: "and in his sizt we monesten oure hertis."

54. La Saincte Bibel (Antwerp, 1530).

55. London reprint, N.T. Domini Nostri J. Chr., Interprete Theodoro Beza (1834).

56. Op. cit., p. 1638. It may be this sense is intended by E. Hunnius (d. 1603), Operum Latinorum, Vol. 4 (Frankfurt, 1606), p. 988, though it is unclear whether he is precisely rendering suadere, or giving the

general meaning as W. Estius (d. 1613) with a supplied
object (Absolutissima in omnes . . . apostolorum Epistolas Commentaria; Rouen, 1709, p. 1232).

57. Gnomon Novi Testamenti (Tübingen, 1742), p. 1054.

58. See Beza's Annotations to N.T. bound up with I.
Tremellius and F. Junius, Testamenti Veteris Biblia
Sacra (Hanover, 1602).

59. Heinrichus Hoogeveen, Doctrinae Particularum
Linguae Graecae, Vol. 2 (Leiden, 1769), De Particula
ὅτι, III.3, p. 883.

60. Op. cit., Tractate VI.3, p. 282.

61. One of the more vehement opponents of the Lutheran view was Simon Episcopius (1583-1643), Opera Theolo-
gica, Vol. 2 (Rotterdam, 1665), p. 341b, who regarded
it not only as contrary to the preceding and subsequent
context, but as falsa et impia, and opposed "to the
whole aim of the Epistle and to the principles of universal religion."

62. One of the earlier Catholic commentaries to
break with the traditional interpretation was A. Bisping, Erklärung der Kath. Briefe (Münster, 1871); he
was followed by J. E. Belser, Die Briefe des hl. Johannes (Freiburg, 1906), pp. 90-2; by Joseph Chaine,
Les Epîtres Catholiques (Paris, 1939), pp. 191-3; by
A, Skrinjar, "Maior est Deus corde nostro," in Verbum
Domini, 20 (1940), pp. 340-50 (in Latin); and by Wil-
libald Lauck, Herders Bibelkommentar: Die heilige
Schrift (Freiburg, 1941), Vol. 13, pp. 498-502.

63. J. A. Neander (E.T.), The First Epistle of John
Practically Explained, tr. H. C. Conant (New York,
1852), p. 222.

64. Matthias Flacius, Novum Testamentum J. Chr.
Filii Dei cum Glossa Compendaria (Frankfurt, 1659; 1st
ed. 1570).

65. Philip Jacob Spener, Des Hochlerleuchteten Apos-
tels und Evangelisten Johannis Erste Epistel . . . er-
klähret (Halle, 1699). His interpretation is very
characteristic: "And therefore he sees not only our
outward circumstances, but also our sinful defects,
not only the reality of our love (as Jn. 21.17) but
also what is hidden and abides in our very hearts,
and therefore the most inward thing in it, faith,
which a man does not feel of himself, but which he

should infer from the fruits of love" (p. 285). I may note that F. Dusterdieck (Die drei Johannischen Briefe, Göttingen, 1854, Vol. 2, p. 207) mentions Sebastian Schmid(t) (1617-96). His Commentarius in Johannis primam Epistolam appeared in Frankfurt, 1707.

66. F. Zoepfl, Didymi Alex, im epistolas canonicas brevis enarratio (Münster, 1914); Latin only. Genuineness disputed, but see K. Staab, "Die griechische Katenenkommentare zu der katholischen Briefen," in Biblica, 5 (1924), pp. 296-353; and R. Devreesse in Dict. de la Bible, Suppl. I (Paris, 1928), col. 1226-7. Fragments from the lost commentaries of Chrysostom and Cyril Alex. (Migne, PG, 64, col. 1059-62 and 74, col. 1022-24) do not gloss our verses. Nor does Cassiodorus, PL, 70, col. 1369-76.

67. But the commentary of Didymus is a witness to the conscience interpretation by giving the text of 3.21 (op. cit., p. 78, line 2) with the two additional ἡμῶν's. See also the excerpt from Cyril Alex. on 3.21 in Cramer, Catenae, Vol. 8, p. 129.

68. J. A. Cramer, Catenae Graecorum Patrum in N.T. (Oxford, 1844), Vol. 8, p. 128. For pseudo-Oecumenius (10th cy.) see Migne, PG, 119, col. 657. This is repeated virtually verbatim in Theophylact (11th cy.), Migne, PG, 126, col. 41.

69. Corpus Scriptorum Christianorum Orien., ed. Chabot, Guidi, Hyvernat: Scriptores Syri (Rome, 1910), Vol. 18 and 20 (old number 101), ed. I. Sedlacek, p. 125.

70. "And by this, we recognise that we are of the truth; and, before he shall come, we make our hearts confident. But if our heart condemneth us, how much greater is God than our hearts, and knowing all things?" James Murdock, op. cit.

71. Op. cit., col. 342.

72. Since it would be tedious to attempt a complete list of those favoring the 'forgiveness' interpretation over against those advocating the rival view of God as 'judging,' I content myself with expanding the list given in J. E. Hunter, E.T. from the 3rd German edition, Critical and Exegetical Handbook to the General Epistles (New York, 1887), p. 573. Some names have been added from Düsterdieck, op. cit., but most from my

own researches. God as forgiving: Nicholas of Gorran
(partly), Hugh of St. Cher (partly), Luther, John Wild,
Flacius, Spener, Sebastian Schmidt, Bengel, J. Lange,
Morus (Düsterdieck, II, p. 207, puts him on the wrong
side), Russmeyer, Moessett, Wolf, Steinhofer, Rickli,
Jachmann, Baumgarten-Crusius, Sander, Mayer, Besser,
Düsterdieck, Erdmann, Myrbert, Ewald, Brückner, Braune,
Bisping, Huther, Westcott, Belser, Brooke, Chaine,
Skrinjar, Lauck, Dodd, Bonsirven, Ambroggi, F. M. Braun,
Stott, Schnackenburg, Bultmann. God as judging: Augus-
tine, Bede, glossa ordinaria, Nicholas of Lyra, Jan
Hus, Dionysius the Carthusian, Cajetan, Tyndale, Oeco-
lampadius, Tittelmans, Bullinger, Calvin, Beza, Socinus,
Arias, Grotius, Salmeron, Lorinus, Cornelius a Lapide,
Castalio, Hornejus, Hunnius, Estius, Episcopius, West-
minster Annotations, Cotton, de la Haye, Pearson,
Poole, Calvius, Calmet, Semler, Lücke, Neander, Ger-
lach, de Wette, Ebrard, Wohlenberg, Findlay, Camerlynck.

73. G. G. Findlay, "Christian Heart Assurance," Expositor (1905), pp. 380-400.

74. Op. cit., in NKZ, 13 (1902), pp. 632-45.

75. A. Camerlynck, Comm. in Epistolas Catholicas
(Brussels, 1909), ad loc.

76. J. de la Haye, Biblia Maxima (Paris, 1660),
Vol. 17, ad loc.

77. A. Calmet, Commentaire littéral sur les Livres
de l'Ancien et Nouveau Testament (Paris, 1724-6), Vol.
8, p. 873.

78. J. E. Belser (op. cit., p. 91) makes clear that
the reproaches of conscience only concern sins already
atoned for by repentance and penance. It is an anxious,
not an outrightly guilty conscience, that John has in
mind. A. Skrinjar (op. cit., p. 346) similarly extends
the notion beyond venial sin, but denies Luther's exegesis so far as it involves an over-scrupulous or
clearly misguided conscience. Rather it is the normal
weakness of conscience which entertains doubts about
its true situation, that is John's concern both here
and wherever he reminds his readers that the blood of
Christ "cleanses from all sin" (1. Jn. 1.7).

79. In The Testament of God 5.3, we have a parallel to the usual rendering of 1 John 20a, 'if our heart

condemn us (ἐὰν καταγινώσκη ἡμῶν ἡ καρδία): (the righteous man) οὐχ ὑπ' ἀλλοῦ καταγινωσόμενεſ ἀλλ' ὑπὸ τῆſ ἰδίαſ καρδίαſ "being condemned not by someone else but by his own heart." I am inclined to think this both is dependent upon, and reflects a misreading of John.

80. The expression which refers backward is ἐκ τούτου (4.6).

81. The passages usually cited to indicate that πείθω in 1 John 3.19 may mean (tranquillize, reassure" are as follows: 2 Mac. 4.45; Mt. 28.14; Mart. Pol. 10.2; Xenephon, Hell. 1.7.7; Anab. 3.1.26. As we have seen, this supposed use of πείθω goes back to Luther and Tyndale.

82. While in Greek the heart is thought of as the seat of the affections, in Hebrew it is primarily the seat of understanding (Ps. 33.11), which includes the will and the moral life, as well as the affections. To "think" is to "say in the heart" (Ps. 14.1). The heart "plans" (Prov. 16.9), "seeks knowledge" (Eccles. 8.16) and "remembers" (Prov. 3.3) as well as "is grieved" (Ps. 73.2), is "broken" (Ps. 51.17), "gathers mischief" (Ps. 41.6) and is "hardened" (Ps. 95.8).

83. See R. Bultmann, Die drei Johannesbriefe (Göttingen, 1967), p. 62; "Analyse des I Joh." in Festgabe für A. Jülicher (Tübingen, 1927), pp. 150f; "Die kirchliche Redaktion des I Joh." in In Memoriam E. Lohmeyer (Stuttgart, 1951), pp. 198-201.

84. E.g., Schnackenburg, op. cit., p. 201, n. 2.

85. For the N.T. use of ὅτι ἐὰν for ὅ τι ἄν , see Col. 3.17; Mk. 6/23 (v. 1). Cf. Acts 3.23 (ἥτιſ ἐάν) and Gal. 5.10 (ὅστιſ ἐάν). For the frequent use in the Koine, see F. Blass-Debrunner, Grammatik des ntl. Griechisch (Göttingen, 1954; 9th ed.) par 107. For ὅ τι ἄν see Jn. 2.5, 14.13, 15.16 and Lk. 10.35. For ὅ ἐάν = ὅ ἄν, see 1 Jn. 3.22, and 5.15 construed as an accusative of respect.

86. It may be that no emphasis is intended. See the order ὑμῶν ἡ καρδία in Jn. 14.1, 27; 16.6, 22; and αὐτοῦ τὸν λόγον in 1 Jn. 2.5.

***

RIGORISM AND LAXISM (Winslow)

1. I am grateful to Lois Young of the Episcopal Divinity School and Lucien Richard of the Weston School of Theology for reading the first draft of this essay and for their helpful criticisms.
2. See Frances Young, "A Cloud of Witnesses," in J. Hick (ed.), The Myth of God Incarnate (London, SCM, 1977), pp. 13-47.
3. See R. C. Gregg and D. E. Groh, "The Centrality of Soteriology in Early Arianism," Anglican Theological Review, 59 (1977), pp. 260-78.
4. See M. F. Wiles, "The Unassumed is the Unhealed," Religious Studies, 4. (1969), pp. 47-56.
5. C. E. Raven, A Wanderer's Way (New York: Holt, 1929), p. 184f.
·6. See, for instance, H. A. Williams, "Incarnation: Model and Symbol," Theology, 79 (1976), pp. 6-18.
7. See Frances Young, Sacrificial Ideas in Greek Christian Writers (Cambridge, Mass.: Philadelphia Patristic Foundation, 1979).

***

IN PRAISE OF THE KING (Schoedel)

*W. H. Auden, The Truest Poetry is the Most Feigning.
1. W. R. Schoedel, "Christian 'Atheism' and the Peace of the Roman Empire," Church History, 42 (1973), 309-19.
2. W. R. Schoedel (ed.), Athenagoras: Legatio and De Resurrectione, "Oxford Early Christian Texts" (Oxford: Clarendon Press, 1972), p. xi.
3. Ibid., pp. xviii-xx. Cf. Nino Scivoletto, "Cultura e scoliastica in Atenagora," Giornale Italiano di Filologia, 13 (1960), 236-48.
4. Schoedel, Athenagoras, pp. xii-xiv and xxiii-xxv. Cf. Michele Pellegrino, Studi su l'antica apologetica (Rome, 1947), pp. 48-85.
5. Conrad Bursian, Der Rhetor Menandros und seine Schriften, in Abhandlungen der philosophisch-philologischen Classe der koniglich Bayerischen Akademie der Wissenschaften, XVI/3 (München, 1882), pp. 1-152. Bursian's text is superior to that of Leonard Spengel,

Rhetores Graeci, III (Leipzig, 1856), pp. 331-446.

6. Bursian (op. cit., pp. 26-8) believes that the chapters are out of order in the manuscripts and assigns this one to the fifth place (in Spengel's ed., pp. 368-77).

7. Especially "Concerning a Public Address" (to a ruler) in Spengel, III, 414-18, and "Concerning a Speech on the Crown" (bestowed on a king) in Spengel, III, 422-3. These are the first and sixth chapters, respectively, in Bursian's edition.

8. Richard Volkmann, Die Rhetorik der Griechen und Römer (Leipzig, 1885), p. 341.

9. André Boulanger, Aelius Aristides (Paris, 1923), pp. 382-4, thinks the 9th oration has as its subject one of the Roman emperors between 192-284 A.D. We use the text and pagination of William Dindorf, Aristides, I (Leipzig, 1829), pp. 98-112.

10. We are indebted primarily to the text and materials provided by Edouard Galletier, Panégyriques Latins, "Collections de universités de France," 3 vols. (Paris, 1949-55). Galletier follows the numbering of E. Baehrens (with one change involving the reversal of the order of the 4th and 5th orations); he includes in parentheses the numbering of Baehrens (which is also that of the Oxford text edited by R. A. B. Mynors in 1964).

11. L. Praviale, "Teoria e prassi del panegirico Bizantino," Emerita, 17 (1949), 72-105.

12. Bursian, op. cit., pp. 17-26 and 28.

13. E. Norden, "Ein Panegyricus auf Augustus in Vergils Aeneis," Rheinisches Museum, N.F. (1899), 466-82.

14. W. Kroll, "Rhetorik," in PWK, Suppl. VII (1940), p. 1132. Cf. Praviale, op. cit., pp. 76-7.

15. References to Menander are given by page and line number of Spengel's edition (S) and also by the paragraph numbers used by Bursian (B).

16. Other themes for the introduction are also allowed by Menander. One of these will be noted later. A clever variation of the usual form is provided by Libanius who declares that though he usually omits the customary remarks about the orator's inability to measure up to so great a task, yet in this instance

(the praise of Constantius and Constans) he feels it
is necessary (Or. 59.5).

17. Early epideictic theory (Kroll, op. cit., pp.
1129-30) provided for orations focussed either on a
person's deeds (historically arranged) or on his "virtues" (organized on philosophical lines). Menander's
theory differs in that the two types have been mixed
and a definite scheme of topics suggested. According
to the older theory (Kroll, op. cit., p. 1130), the
tone of epideictic is determined by "amplification"
(auxesis) and "comparison." The former becomes dominant
in the later theory (Praviale, op. cit., pp. 80-3).

18. Well summarized by Martin Dibelius, Die Pastoral-
briefe, "Handbuch zum N.T.," 13 (2nd ed., Tübingen,
1931), pp. 22-5. Tertullian gives the fullest list of
topics included in such prayers: long life, security
to the empire, protection of the imperial house, brave
armies, a faithful senate, a virtuous people, peace
(Apol. 30.3).

19. We are dependent above all on the text, translation, and study by James H. Oliver, The Ruling Power,
in Transactions of the American Philosophical Society,
N.S. 43/4 (Philadelphia, 1953), pp. 871-1003.

20. Robert M. Grant, Augustus to Constantine (New
York, 1970), p. 92.

21. Oliver, op. cit., pp. 873-86.

22. Op. cit., p. 879. Cf. Volkmann, op. cit., pp.
334-5 (in his praise of cities, Aristides follows a
scheme not unlike that found in the first treatise
that goes under the name of Menander).

23. According to the first treatise that comes down
to us under the name of Menander, "panygyrics on cities
are mixtures of topics about countries and about men;
for from those about countries one should take the topic of setting; and from those about men the topics of
race, deeds, practices; for on the basis of these we
praise cities" (346.27-347.1 S; 1 B). Quintilian already indicates that "cities are eulogized in the same
way as persons" (Inst. 3.7.26). Bursian theorizes that
our first Menandrian treatise lacks a chapter on the
praise of men because the two topics--cities and men--
overlapped so much (op. cit., p. 21).

24. Schoedel, Athenagoras, pp. xi-xii.

25. The source and significance of Athenagoras' views on the political use of religion are discussed in my "Christian 'Atheism' and the Peace of the Roman Empire," cited above, n. 2.

26. William Tern, Hellenistic Civilization, 3rd ed., rev. by Tarn and Griffith (London, 1952), p. 53.

27. Oliver, op. cit., p. 880. By Athenagoras' day, the legal distinction between the honestiores and humiliores was a fact of life. There is undeniably a measure of artificiality in the continued emphasis on equality before the law after the time of Antoninus Pius in whose reign one finds "the earliest imperial constitution which recognizes the distinction" (Oliver, p. 921). Like Menander, Aelius Aristides stresses the equal treatment of the poor and rich, the low and high born.

28. Oliver, op. cit., p. 1003.

29. Op. cit., p. 889.

30. Op. cit., p. 890.

31. Martin P. Nilsson, in his Geschichte der griechischen Religion, II (München, 1950), p. 371, n. 1, quotes an interesting inscription from Halicarnassus from the time of Augustus: ". . . the eternal and immortal Nature of the Universe granted the greatest good unto men with a view to abundant blessings by bringing Caesar Augustus into our happy life--the father of his fatherland, the goddess Rome, paternal Zeus and Savior of the whole human race, whose providence not only fulfilled the prayers of all but also more than fulfilled them. For the earth and the sea are at peace, the cities flourish with good laws, like-mindedness and blessing abound, all good matures and bears fruit. Men are filled with good hopes for the future and confidence for the present . . ."

32. Bursian's text.

33. Bursian's text.

34. Johannes A. Straub, Vom Herrscherideal in der Spätantike (Stuttgart, 1964), pp. 171-2.

35. Bursian's text.

36. See Straub (op. cit., pp. 121-4), who refers in particular to Pan. Lat. vi (7), 14. Eusebius finds a parallel between God and his Word on the one hand and

the emperor and his Caesars on the other; the Latin
Panegyrist describes Maximianus as directing the empire "with a celestial nod" from on high and Constantine as actively traversing the empire (the comparison
with lesser gods or daemons is implied).

37. Bursian's text (tolma). Spengel reads "honor
(time) concerning the king." The more unusual term also makes sense, however, and is to be preferred. "Boldness" (tolma) was regarded as an important virtue for
the rhetorician (Dionys, Halicarn., De Isocr. 1). And
Aelius Aristides concludes his oration on Rome with the
remark, "my bold attempt (tolmema) is finished" (109).
Thus "boldness concerning the king" is to be understood
as a forthright effort to praise matters of such moment-
ous significance.

38. Cf. A. H. M. Jones, The Later Roman Empire (Oxford, 1964), I, 321.

39. See Praviale, op. cit., pp. 76-7, and the studies cited there (Schanz, Geffcken, Burckhardt, Pichon,
Leclerq).

40. Straub, op. cit., pp. 146-59.

41. Op. cit., pp. 148-51.

42. Op. cit., pp. 153-9.

43. Op. cit., pp. 160-74.

44. Chester G. Starr, Civilization and the Caesars:
The Intellectual Revolution in the Roman Empire (Itha-
ca, N.Y., 1954), pp. 147-68.

45. Schoedel, "Christian 'Atheism,'" pp. 318-9.

46. Oliver, op. cit., p. 889.

47. Op. cit., p. 892.

***

MARCION'S JEALOUS GOD (Muehlenberg)

1. A. von Harnack, Marcion: das Evangelium vom fremden Gott, 2nd ed., 1924 (reprint, 1960); cited by page
reference only.

2. Ibid., p. 169.

3. U. Bianchi, "Marcion: Théologien biblique ou doc-
teur gnostique?" Vigiliae Christianae, 21 (1967), pp.
141-9.

4. F. M. Braun, "Marcion et la gnose simonienne," Byzantion, 25-7 (1955-7), pp. 632-48.

5. B. Aland, "Marcion: Versuch einer neuen Interpretation," Zeitschrift für Theologie und Kirche, 70 (1973), pp. 420-47.

6. In Zeitschrift für Kirchengeschichte, 40 (1922), p. 204.

7. Advsersus Marcionem V.13.4. I quote according to the sub-paragraph of Ernest Evans' edition (Tertullian: Adversus Marcionem, 1972) and acknowledge the use of his translation although I do not indicate where I have departed from it.

8. Cf. Harnack, p. 252* and 261.*

9. Adamantius, Dial. II.17 should not be trusted.

10. Cf. Harnack, pp. 268*-269* for references.

11. Cf. II.29.4 and IV.1.11.

12. Cf. Comm. III.6 in Rom. (Harnack pp. 260*-261*).

13. J. G. Gager, "Marcion and Philosophy," Vigiliae Christianae, 26 (1972), pp. 53-9.

14. Cf. Aland, op. cit., p. 439 for references.

15. Irenaeus, Adv. haer, I.27.2.

16. Cf. Braun, op. cit.

17. Adv. haer, I.23.3.

18. Cf. K. Beyschlag, Simon Magus und die christliche Gnosis (1974), pp. 203-10, esp. p. 208, n. 144.

19. There is perhaps a more specific relationship between aemulatio and the topos of divine envy; cf. W. C. Van Unnik, ΑΦΘΩΝΩΣ ΜΕΤΑΔΙΔΩΜΙ, Mededelingen van de Koninklijke Vlaamse Academie voor Wetenschappen, Letteren en Schone Kunsten van Belgie, Klasse der Letteren (Brussels, 1971; Jaargang 1971, nr. 4) and "De ἀφθονία van God in de oudchristelijke literatuur," Mededelingen der Koninklijke Nederlandse Akademie van Wetenschappen, Afd. Letterkunde 36, No. 2 (Amsterdam, 1973).

20. See note 4 supra.

21. Cf. S. Pètrement, "La Mythe des sept archontes créateurs," Le Origini del Gnosticismo (Colloquio di Messina, 1967), pp. 460-86.

22. Cf. Braun, op. cit., pp. 647-8.

23. Cf. H. Jonas, Gnosis und spätantiker Geist (2nd ed., 1954), Part I, p. 208, n. 1.

24. Cf. M. Pohlenz, Die Stoa: Geschichte einer geistigen Bewegung (2nd ed., 1955), Vol. 2, p. 198.

25. J. Woltmann, "Der geschichtliche Hintergrund der Lehre Markions vom 'Fremden Gott,'" E. Suttner and C. Patak (ed.), Wegzeichen. Festgabe zum 60. Geburtstag von Prof. Dr. M. H. Biedermann (1971), pp. 15-42.

26. Cf. my paper, "Verité et bonté de Dieu. Une interpretation de 'De incarnatione,' chapitre VI, en perspective historique," C. Kannengiesser (ed.), Politique et Théologie chez Athanase d'Alexandrie (1974), pp. 215-30.

***

PLENITUDO HUMANITATIS (Balas)

*This article is a slightly revised version of a paper presented at the annual meeting of the American Society of Church History (San Francisco, Dec., 1973). At that time I was not yet acquainted with the valuable article of K. B. Skouteris, "The Unity of Human Nature as Actual Presupposition of Salvation" (in Greek), reprinted from Θεολογία (1969). In my judgment, the author does not distinguish sufficiently the two different "models" of unity found in Gregory. Since then, Reinhard M. Hübners long awaited study has been finally published: Die Einheit des Leibes Christi bei Gregor von Nyssa: Untersuchungen zum Ursprung der 'physischen' Erlösungslehre, Philosophia Patrum, Vol. II (Leiden: E. J. Brill, 1974). Although Professor Hübner's interpretation of Gregory's thought differs from mine in several respects, I am still convinced of the correctness of my brief synthesis. I hope to discuss his views in detail elsewhere.

1. H. C. Baldry, The Unity of Mankind in Greek Thought (Cambridge: Univ. Press, 1965), p. 1.

2. For a general review of the state of studies on Gregory of Nyssa, see W. Volker, Gregor von Nyssa als Mystiker (Wiesbaden, 1955), pp. 1-22; my Metousia Theou: Man's Participation in God's Perfections according to St. Gregory of Nyssa (Rome, 1966), pp. 14-18; J. Daniélou, "Orientations actuelles de la recherche sur Grégoire de Nysse," Ecriture et culture philosophique dans

la pensée de Grégoire de Nysse (Leiden, 1971), pp. 3-17. In the bibliographies of these books one can find information on monographic studies referred to in these notes. H. De Lubac's magnificent synthesis Catholicisme: Les aspects sociaux du dogme (5th ed., Paris, 1952) (E.T.: Catholicism: A Study of Dogma in Relation to the Corporate Destiny of Mankind) contains many references to Gregory of Nyssa; underlying philosophical conceptions, however, are not analyzed.

3. Ad Abl.: GNO (= Gregorii Nysseni Opera) III, 1, p. 40, 5-41, 12; E.T.: LCC (= Library of Christian Classics), Vol. III, pp. 257-8. The works of Gregory will be referred to in this paper acc. to the critical edition inaugurated by W. Jaeger; for works not yet published there, reference will be to Migne, PG, Vols. 44-46, except for the Or. cat., ed. by J. H. Srawley (Cambridge, 1956).

4. For references, see my paper "Participation in the Specific Nature according to Gregory of Nyssa," in Actes du Quatrième Congrès Internationale de Philosophie Médiévale (Paris, 1969), pp. 1079-85.

5. Cf., e.g., C. Eun. I.279-93 (GNO I, pp. 105-13), analyzed in my Met. Theou, pp. 54-63.

6. De hom. op. 16: (PG 44:185B-D), E.T.: NPNF V, p. 406 (corrected).

7. E. Corsini, "Plérôme humain et plérôme cosmique chez Grégoire de Nysse," in Ecriture et culture, pp. 111-26.

8. Art. cit., p. 122.

9. For the meaning of the term in general, see G. Delling, "πλῆθοσ, etc.," Theol. Wörterbuch zum N. T., 6 (1959), pp. 274-82 and Ibid., "πλήρησ, etc.," pp. 283-309; J. Ernst, Pleroma und Pleroma Christi (Regensburg, 1970); Lampe, A Patristic Greek Lexicon, s.v.

10. Cf. Met. Theou, index s.v.

11. Cf. e.g., De hom. op. 22: (PG 44:205A).

12. Cf. e.g., In Hex.: (PG 44:113C).

13. Cf. e.g., De an. et res.: (PG 46:128B).

14. I use the terms theologia and oikonomia in the sense in which Gregory uses them, e.g., in Or. cat., the former referring to the doctrine of the Triune God, the latter to the divine dispensation of salvation history.

15. Cf. Met. Theou, pp. 23-33.

16. De or. dom. 5: (PG 44:1184A-1185A); E.T.: ACW, 18, pp. 76-7.

17. A von Harnack, Lehrbuch der Dogmengeschichte, II (Darmstadt, 1964; 4th ed.), p. 166. See also J. Pelikan, The Christian Tradition, I (Chicago, 1971), p. 128.

18. Ibid., p. 165.

19. Or. cat. 32 (Srawley, pp. 115,15-117,9); E.T.: LCC, III, p. 310.

20. Harnack, op. cit., p. 166.

21. Ibid., p. 165.

22. Cf. Met. Theou, pp. 76-99: "The Partaking of Divine Life."

23. On the meaning of this term in Gregory, see R. Hübner, "Gregor von Nyssa und Markell von Ankyra," in Ecriture et culture, pp. 199-299.

24. Cf. Met. Theou, pp. 151-2.

25. Cf. esp. De an. et res.: (PG 44:126-60).

26. Cf. my paper, "Eternity and Time in Gregory of Nyssa's Contra Eunomium," given at the II International Gregory of Nyssa Colloquy (Frackenhorst bei Münster/Westf., 1972), to be published in the Proceedings of the Colloquy.

27. Cf. e.g., J. Daniélou, "L'apocatastase chez Grégoire de Nysse," Recherches de Science Religieuse, 48 (1940), pp. 328-47, and his L'être et le temps chez Grégoire de Nysse (Leiden, 1970), pp. 205-66; also his "Metempsychosis in Gregory of Nyssa," in The Heritage of the Early Church, Orient. Christ. Anal., Vol. 15 (Rome, 1973), pp. 227-43.

28. Cf. P. Sherwood, The Earlier Ambigua of St. Maximus the Confessor and his Refutation of Origenism (Rome, 1955), pp. 205-22.

29. I have treated Irenaeus' views in detail in an as yet unpublished paper entitled "Participation and Communion in the Adversus Haereses of St. Irenaeus."

30. Peri archon IV.4.9 (ed. Koetschau, pp. 361-2).

31. Cf. Baldry, op. cit., pp. 151ff.

32. Cf. J. Lebon, "Le sort de 'Consubstantiel' nicéen," Revue d'Histoire Ecclésiastique, 47 (1952), pp. 485-529 and 48 (1953), pp. 632-82. On the relationship between Basil and Gregory, see my paper, "The Unity of

Hunan Nature in Basil'a and Gregory of Nyssa's Polemics against Eunomius," presented at the VI International Conference on Patristic Studies (Oxford, Sept., 1971) and to be published in the Proceedings.

33. Cf. Commentaria in Aristotelem Graeca IV, 1: Porphyrius, Isagoge et in Categorias Commentarium, ed. A. Busse (Berlin, 1887), index, s.v.

34. Epist. de Incarnatione Verbi: S. Anselmi . . . Opera Omnia, ed. F. S. Schmitt (Edinburgh, 1946), Vol. II, p. 10.

35. For the state of the question as to the influence of Gregory of Nyssa on John Eriugena, see my as yet unpublished paper given at the Medieval Conference in Kalamazoo, April, 1973.

36. Cf. e.g., Gregory's homily, "In illus, quando sibi subjecerit omnia": (PG 44:1305-1326).

37. Cf. e.g., F. Flückiger, Geschichte des Naturrechtes, I: Altertum und Erühmittelalter (Zollikon-Zurich, 1954) which is, however, far from comprehensive.

38. Cf, e.g., F. Dvornik, Early Christian and Byzantine Political Philosophy, 2 vols. (Washington, D.C., 1966).

***

STRUCTURAL ANALYSIS OF SALVATION (Laeuchli)

1. Robert C. Gregg and Dennis E. Groh, "The Centrality of Soteriology in Early Arianism," Anglican Theological Review, 59 (1977), pp. 260-278.

2. Donald F. Winslow, "Soteriological Orthodoxy in the Fathers," a paper presented to the VII International Conference on Patristic Studies, Oxford, Sept. 1975, to be published in the Proceedings of the Conference.

3. Se my Power and Sexuality: The Emergence of Canon Law at the Synod of Elvira, Philadelphia: Temple Univ. Press, 1972.

RETURN TO THE DIVINE (Tripolitis)

1. This essay is based upon portions of my doctoral dissertation, The Doctrine of the Soul in the Thought of Plotinus and Origen (University of Pennsylvania, 1971).
2. Enn. IV.4:15ff; Princ. I.4:3-5.
3. Enn. IV.7:15; cf. IV.3:5; 4:14-5; I.1:10; II.9:2.
4. Princ. II.9:2.
5. Princ. I.1:4-7; Comm. Jo. I.20ff; C. Cels. IV.14.
6. Comm. Jo. XIII.25.
7. Princ. IV.4:9-10; Comm. Jo. I.34; II.3; VI.38.
8. C. Cels. IV.30; Princ. III.6:1; Comm. Jo. XX.20.
9. Ex. Martyr. 47; C. Cels. VI.63; Princ. IV.4:9-10.
10. Enn. IV.3:5, 8:4; V.1:1-2; Princ. II.9:1, 6; IV.4:9.
11. Enn. IV.8:1, 5.
12. This point is developed further in the dissertation.
13. Princ. II.9:2.
14. Ibid.
15. Enn. I.6:8; IV.9:4, 8; Comm. Jo. II.3; Princ. III.6:1; IV.4:9-10.
16. Enn. II.9:2.
17. Ibid., IV.8:8; V.1:10; VI.4:14.
18. Ibid., V.6:5; VI.7:22, 31, 35.
19. Ibid., I.6:8ff; VI.5:1, 9:4-8.
20. Ibid., VI.7:39.
21. Ibid., VI.7:35-6, 9:4, 11.
22. Ibid., I.6:8; IV.3:6; V.1:1.
23. Ibid., VI.9:4.
24. Princ. IV.4:9-10; Ex. Martyr. 47; C. Cels. VI.63.
25. Especially in Comm. Cant. and the 27th Homily on Numbers.
26. Ex. Martyr. 47; Princ. II.11:4ff; cf. Comm. Cant. I and Enn. VI.7:31.
27. Comm. Cant. II (Koetschau ed., p. 141).
28. C. Cels. VII.42ff; cf. IV.50 and Comm. Cant. II (ed. cit., p. 143ff).
29. C. Cels. VII.33, 43-4; Princ. IV.4:9-10.
30. Hom. Num. XXVII.1-13; Hom. Gen. I.7, 13; Comm. Cant. II (ed. cit., p. 157), III (p. 186). A detailed discussion of the stages of the soul's ascent in the thought of Origen is found in Ch. 7 of the dissertation.

31. <u>C. Cels</u>. I.9ff; VI.2; VII.42-3, 46, 49. 60.
32. Ibid., I.9; VI.2; VII.47, 59-61.
33. <u>Symposium</u>, 203Bff.
34. <u>Enn</u>. VI.7:34, 9:9; <u>Comm. Cant</u>. Prol. (ed. cit.,
p. 65ff).
35. <u>Enn</u>. VI.9:10ff; <u>Comm. Cant</u>. III (ed. cit., pp.
216-28).
36. <u>Enn</u>. VI.7:34; cf. VI.7:35-6, 9:10-11; IV.8:1.
37. <u>Ibid</u>.
38. Ibid., VI.9:10.
39. <u>Princ</u>. III.6:3; <u>Comm. Cant</u>. III (ed. cit., p.
225ff).
40. <u>Hom. Cant</u>. I.7; <u>Comm. Cant</u>. III (p. 218).
41. <u>Princ. III</u>.6:3; cf. <u>Comm. Cant</u>. III (p. 218).
42. <u>Princ</u>. III.6:1-3; cf. <u>II.11:7</u>.

***

SOTERIOLOGICAL COMMONPLACES IN CYRIL (McInerney)

1. The references throughout are to Pusey's edition
of the works of Cyril (Oxford, 1872) and indicate chapter and verse of the Gospel text.
2. One of the propositions which Cyril attacks in
this commentary is definitely Origenist, and not Arian,
i.e., the pre-existence of souls and their fall (1.9).
Another Origenist position refuted is the doctrine of
satiation and additional falls (7.24).

LIST OF CONTRIBUTORS

ROBERT A. KRAFT is professor of religious studies
(Hellenistic Religions, Judaism, and Christianity),
chairman of the department, and coördinator of
graduate studies in religion at the University of
Pennsylvania, Philadelphia.

VAN A. HARVEY, formerly chairman of the Department of
Religious Studies at the University of Pennsylvania, is currently professor of religious studies
at Stanford University.

CYRIL C. RICHARDSON was Washburn Professor-Emeritus
of Church History at Union Theological Seminary
in New York City. He died in November of 1976
at the age of sixty-seven.

DONALD F. WINSLOW is professor of historical theology
at the Episcopal Divinity School in Cambridge,
Massachusetts, and is co-founder of the Philadelphia Patristic Foundation.

WILLIAM R. SCHOEDEL is professor of classics and religious studies at the University of Illinois,
Urbana, Illinois. He was formerly on the faculty
of Brown University.

EKKEHARD MUEHLENBERG, prior to accepting his present
position as professor of church history at the
University of Göttingen, was on the faculty of
the School of Theology at Claremont, California.

DAVID L. BALAS, O. Cist., is professor of theology
at the University of Dallas in Irving, Texas.

SAMUEL LAEUCHLI is professor of religion, specializ-
ing in patristics, at Temple University in Philadelphia.

211

ANTONIA TRIPOLITIS is assistant professor in classics at Douglass College, Rutgers University, in New Brunswick, New Jersey.

JOSEPH LEE McINERNEY, a former graduate student in re-- ligious studies at the University of Pennsylvania, is an ordained minister of the Episcopal Church.

D 3566078